the
ART PLAYROOM

the
ART PLAYROOM

make a home art space for kids

Megan Schiller

founder of The Art Pantry

spark
exploration,
independence, and
joyful learning
with invitations
to create

QUARRY

Quarto.com

© 2023 Quarto Publishing Group USA Inc.
Text, Photos © 2023 Megan Schiller

First Published in 2023 by Quarry Books, an imprint of The Quarto Group,
100 Cummings Center, Suite 265-D, Beverly, MA 01915, USA.
T (978) 282-9590   F (978) 283-2742

Quarry Books titles are also available at discount for retail, wholesale, promotional, and bulk purchase. For details, contact the Special Sales Manager by email at specialsales@quarto.com or by mail at The Quarto Group, Attn: Special Sales Manager, 100 Cummings Center, Suite 265-D, Beverly, MA 01915, USA.

10 9 8 7 6 5 4 3 2 1

ISBN: 978-0-7603-8134-2

Digital edition published in 2023
eISBN: 978-0-7603-8135-9

Library of Congress Cataloging-in-Publication Data

Names: Schiller, Megan, author.
Title: The Art Playroom : Make a Home Art Space for Kids / Megan Schiller, founder of The Art Pantry.
Description: Beverly, MA : Quarry Books, [2023] | Includes index. |
   Summary: "The Art Playroom is a guide for setting up at-home art spaces and introducing art prompts to promote innovative thinking, skill-building, collaboration, and independence"—Provided by publisher.
Identifiers: LCCN 2022061739 (print) | LCCN 2022061740 (ebook) | ISBN 9780760381342 (trade paperback) | ISBN 9780760381359 (ebook)
Subjects: LCSH: Children's rooms. | Playrooms. | Artists' materials. | Creative ability. | Creative activities and seat work.
Classification: LCC NK2117.C4 S34 2023 (print) | LCC NK2117.C4 (ebook) | DDC 643/.55--dc23/eng/20230105
LC record available at https://lccn.loc.gov/2022061739
LC ebook record available at https://lccn.loc.gov/2022061740

Design and Page Layout: Lisa M. Kelsey Design
Photography: Megan Schiller, unless otherwise noted

Printed in China

To Karuna and Ora, without you there would be no book!
You are my inspiration every day, my life, my loves. May your lives be forever
bursting with creativity, like our many family canvases.

CONTENTS

PREFACE

During my first year as a parent, I knew I wanted to expose my daughter to art and creativity, just as it was exposed to me growing up. My grandmother was an artist, my father is an artist, my older brother is an artist, and I am an artist. As young kids, we were surrounded by visual art and were allowed free access to creative supplies. When we visited our grandmother (which was quite often), we had free rein of her art studio where we spent hours exploring her diverse collection of art supplies. When I was in college, before she passed away, she asked me if there was anything of hers that I wanted to keep. The only thing I wanted was her set of rubber stamps that I had been obsessed with as a little girl.

I also remember how our parents let us "decorate" our bedroom walls. As young kids, we used pencil and crayon on the walls and then graduated to painting murals in our bedrooms as we got older. We were taught to use power tools and were allowed to alter or create our own furniture to suit our needs. This freedom might have been a little over the top for many families, but I always had the confidence that I could create anything that I wanted.

This is why I set out to make artistic exploration part of our daily lives with young children. When my eldest daughter was eighteen months old, I set up an art playroom in our back cottage and began teaching art to the neighborhood kids. After moving the classes to a commercial space, our home playroom took over various corners of the house before finally settling in our converted porch, just off the living room. It holds a prominent position in our small home because we have made art a priority. My curious toddler—who inspired so much of the work that I do—is now fifteen years old. My younger daughter is eleven, and they have grown up with a creative confidence that will stay with them throughout their lives.

In my work, I am dedicated to helping other families bring more creativity into children's lives. As a Reggio Emilia-inspired art teacher, I loved exposing my students to a variety of artistic explorations. It was incredible to watch them develop a creative confidence and move around the playroom, using tools and materials with curiosity and assurance.

When I decided to take a break from teaching art classes so that I could stay home with my second child, the next logical step for me was to help bring this creative experience into children's homes. For the past eleven years, I have worked one-on-one with clients to design art spaces in their homes and schools. But this is not enough. I want to reach more families than is possible with a one-on-one service, so I have written this book for you to tackle it on your own.

This book offers all of the insights that I have learned over two decades of working with kids in creative settings. I share the reasons why developing creative confidence is important for kids and how access to art supplies and open-ended artistic explorations are essential to this development. I then take you through my design process and give you every tip and trick in my tool belt to create an engaging art space for your children. Once your art space is ready to go, I then show you how to introduce your children to new materials and how to set up a variety of art prompts to jumpstart their creative exploration.

PART 1

THE ART SPACE

CHAPTER 1
Why an Art Playroom?

An art playroom is simply a dedicated space with accessible art supplies that allow for open-ended exploration. This art space can be as small as a shoebox, or as large as an entire room—and is often everything in between! The name of my business, The Art Pantry, comes from my belief that an art space is as essential to children's development as a healthy kitchen pantry. Just like a healthy kitchen pantry is stocked with nutritious food and ingredients, a child's home should be stocked with tools and materials for creative nourishment. This art space then becomes a child's workshop, where they can access these tools and materials to work through ideas, tinker, discover, solve problems, learn techniques, and create anything they can imagine. An art playroom is about going back to the basics and allowing children the opportunity to explore with open-ended materials. This encourages children to be creative thinkers and problem solvers while fostering self-confidence and independence.

ART AS A TOOL FOR LEARNING

As parents, we dedicate plenty of living space to our children's toys. Sometimes, we even dedicate an entire room to toys in the hopes of enriching our children's lives through play.

What if we put as much emphasis on art supplies and creative tools as we do on toys?

What if our kids were just as confident and skilled at using artistic materials as they are at building block towers and playing dress-up? This doesn't mean that they would grow up to become the next Picasso, but rather that they would grow up with a creative confidence and an understanding that these tools can be used to enhance other areas of their play.

To achieve this, we have to make art a priority in our homes. We have to make space in our children's lives for more creativity. This means making physical space in our homes, making time in our busy schedules, and opening up to new perspectives on creativity and art. As very young children, toddlers like to explore the world around them. When given the freedom to explore in their own way, all toddlers are curious about creative tools and materials. As kids get older, we tend to segment learning into subject matter and these creative materials are pushed into the discipline of art. If a child doesn't relate to the way that "art" is taught, he begins to shy away from this subject area, eventually seeing it as separate, as something that is only for "creative people." Adults, who also learned to regard art in this way, tend to reinforce this perspective. Art then becomes an elective, rather than a tool for learning and self-expression.

This book is about setting up a space for creating visual art, but it is within the broad goal of helping children to become self-sufficient makers and innovative thinkers. Art is a means of expression, of working out ideas and emotions. It adds an aesthetic beauty to our world, but it is also an essential instrument of learning. While engaged in the creative process, children are continuously problem solving and coming to new conclusions about the way things work. This is why creativity is essential to innovation and is widely accepted as one of the most important skills in life and in the workplace. If we can reshape our views around art and creativity, we can start our kids early on this path of creative thinking and doing—a path of tapping into their intrinsic creative nature and nourishing it. We can help our children feel confident in their creative abilities, foster these fundamental skills, and support the unique ways in which they weave creative thinking into their lives.

Photo Credit: Catalina Gutierrez

"But My Kid Isn't Artistic"

A friend once told me that she didn't do much art with her two boys. When I asked her why, she responded, "When I used to give my son crayons, all he did was use them to build a tower and knock it over." Because her son didn't respond by drawing with the crayons, she assumed he wasn't artistic. But he was being artistic! He was using the materials in a creative way by building a structure and investigating what happens when he knocks it down. What if, rather than avoiding art from that point on, she had nurtured these explorations and continued to provide a variety of artistic materials, adapting to his interests and creative style?

WHAT SKILLS DO KIDS LEARN FROM OPEN-ENDED ART?

Over the past thirteen years, we've had a dedicated space for creating in our home. My kids do a lot of painting, drawing, and crafting, of course, but I've learned over the years that an art space is about so much more than just art. An art space is really more like a workshop or a science lab.

An art space is a place where kids explore materials, investigate ideas, experiment with ingredients, learn new skills, work together, build things, and make astonishing discoveries!

Throughout the years, my kids have used our art space to write stories and songs, they've made gifts and birthday cards, they've built their own toys, they've made family board games, they've made musical instruments, they've learned to share resources, they've discovered solutions to problems . . . I could go on and on. What I love most is that my kids have become resourceful, expressive, collaborative, and confident creators in this art space.

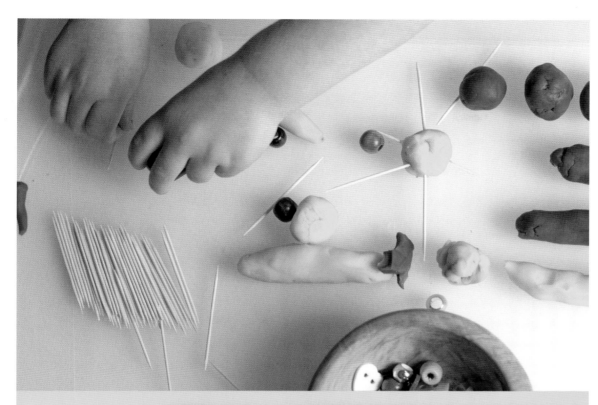

What skills do kids learn from open-ended art?

- Creative thinking
- Critical thinking
- Confidence
- Perseverance
- Collaboration
- Risk-taking
- Hand-eye coordination
- Focus
- Imagination
- Communication
- Appreciation of others
- Muscle control/fine motor

How do these skills play out on a daily basis?

- Reading
- Writing
- Attention span
- Relationships
- Motor development
- Self-esteem
- Leadership

THE INFLUENCE OF ART OVER THE YEARS

BY BARBARA RUCCI OF *ART BAR BLOG* AND THE CREATIVITY PROJECT

I started thinking about my art room the day I found out I was having a baby. Long before Pinterest, I would tear pages out of magazines and keep them in a folder. I called that folder "In My Dreams."

We moved out of our apartment and into a house when my daughter was one. At this age, I introduced her to markers and paper but kept the supplies out of reach. I slowly offered her new experiences, like painting with tempera on an easel, using glue, and making homemade playdough. I kept simple supplies out on a tray, and kept the paints in a closet.

When she was five and had a two-year-old sister, we renovated our house and I finally got the art room I had always dreamed about. It was right off the kitchen, with sliding glass doors to keep the mess contained. It had a sink, a low, round table in the middle, and shelves covering one wall. I hung their finished art on a clothesline across the room.

By the time we moved into this new art room (dream room), most supplies were out in the open for them to use. I rotated them every few weeks to keep it fresh. My kids, the neighborhood kids, play dates, cousins—they were all allowed to help themselves to our supplies and create art whenever they felt inspired. I often left out "invitations" for them to explore. Whether it was watercolors and an interesting shaped paper, or just new markers and small notecards, they always had the choice what to make and explore their creativity.

Now my oldest is twenty-two, and we have moved two more times. Gone is my dream room, but I have learned to create dream corners and dream nooks. I still keep art supplies out, and my children still make things when they are home, taking out paper and markers to make a card, or finding cardboard and hot glue to make a contraption. All three of my children have each found their calling elsewhere, but they have learned some valuable and lifelong lessons from being exposed to art and creativity throughout their childhood. They've learned that mistakes are often an opportunity to try a new direction. They've learned that everyone is different and has his own way of doing things, but each person has value and can use some encouragement. They've learned to appreciate aesthetics and recognize when something is designed well. And most of all, they are playful, creative thinkers who aren't afraid of trying new things.

As their mom, it makes me feel like all those years of putting out supplies and cleaning them up had a deeper value than I ever thought. I've also realized that children really don't need much to reach their full, creative potential. Just some simple supplies, a space to call their own, and the freedom to express themselves without grown-up expectations.

Photo Credit: Barbara Rucci

This toddler art space is located in an open-concept living room/kitchen in the center of the home. My client wanted the design to blend in with the playful, contemporary look of the rest of the room while also being inviting and appropriate for a toddler.

A mix of clear containers with woven and wood materials and pops of color allow the art supplies to take center stage while still maintaining a soothing and organized design.

DESIGN MATTERS

How do you feel when you are cooking in a messy kitchen, or working at a cluttered desk? Is it enjoyable, or does it stress you out? What if you were making dinner and your cooking tools were misplaced and broken? This same feeling applies to children's art spaces. Whether it's your child's art space, your hall closet, your workspace, or your kitchen cabinets, a well-organized area makes you feel at ease and ready to use the space. Design has the ability to affect our mood and productivity and is, therefore, a key factor in educational spaces. Your art space, no matter how small, is an educational space. If it's accessible, organized, aesthetically pleasing, and filled with quality materials, your child will be drawn to it. Don't be surprised if you are suddenly drawn to it too!

CHAPTER 2

Setting Up Your Art Playroom

Ready to set up your art space? Let's get started! Setting up an art space for your child may sound daunting, but I am here to help. If you follow this process, you will end up with an organized and inviting art space, adapted to suit the needs of your home and family.

Investing some time, energy, and resources into your art space now will lay the foundation for years of creative exploration. If this process ever feels overwhelming, you can always start with a simple plan and layer in additional furniture, containers, or supplies as needed.

WHAT MATERIALS AND TOOLS SHOULD BE IN AN ART PLAYROOM?

Before we get into designing the space, it's important to know what kind of art supplies you will want to include. Some people believe that children's art supplies should be as cheap as possible because they go through them quickly and might ruin them. I have a different outlook. I believe that when you offer children quality materials—and teach them how to take care of them—they will feel important and respected and will rise to the occasion (most likely with some reminders!). High quality supplies also offer brighter pigments and last longer. This doesn't mean they have to be expensive. There are a variety of affordable brands that offer high quality art supplies for children. The amount and variety of materials will depend on the size of your space. If your art space is the size of a shoebox, you can start with a few of the essentials, and then change them out every once in a while, for a new medium. If you have a large space, you can include some or all of the "extra goodies" in addition to the essentials.

PRODUCT TIP
Trays make everything easier. Art trays are the most used item in our playroom. We use them for containing messy projects as well as for transporting everything to the sink for clean-up. I can't stress enough how essential trays have become in our space.

PRODUCT TIP
For paint cups, you can purchase spill-proof cups with lids and paint palettes, or you can use items that you already have, like plastic dishes, muffin tins, or ice cube trays.

A few of the essential supplies.

Essentials

Art trays: Any large sturdy tray will do (kitchen tray, cookie sheet, or tray from an art supply shop)

Drawing tools:
- Markers: Fine and broad
- Crayons (beeswax is best for bold and easy marks)
- Colored pencils (not essential for under age 5) and pencil sharpener

Paints and accessories:
- Watercolor paints
- Tempera paint
- Paint brushes, chubby and fine
- Paint cups (nonspill paint cups with lids are great)

Paper:
- Drawing paper
- Paint paper

Glue:
- White school glue
- Glue sticks

Tape:
- Scotch tape on a stand
- Masking tape

Printmaking:
- Stamps and stamp pad (washable stamp pad for young children)

Cutting tools:
- Scissors: Child-sized (ages 1.5 to 3, use plastic, safety scissors that only cut paper)

Modeling:
- Playdough
- Tools (roller, hammer, cutter, cookie cutter—a popsicle stick can work as a cutting tool)

Collage:
- Random bits of items (sequins, buttons, googly eyes, beads, small paper pieces, pom poms, etc.)

Natural items (twigs, branches, leaves, acorns, shells, rocks, etc.)

SAFETY FIRST
Make sure to purchase only art supplies that are explicitly made for children, so you can be assured that they are nontoxic. Also be aware of any safety labels, like choking hazards for young children.

A few of the "extra goodies."

Extra Goodies (and Fun Additions for Older Children)

- Apron
- Table cover
- Spill mat for floor
- Construction paper
- Origami paper
- Glitter
- Glitter paint
- Glitter glue
- Wood glue (ages 3+)
- Acrylic paint (for older kids and/or supervised special projects)
- Liquid watercolors
- Oil pastels (made specifically for kids so they are nontoxic)
- Chalk pastels
- Fabric markers
- Paint markers
- Chalkboard/sidewalk chalk
- Duct tape (ages 5+)
- Colored masking tape or decorative craft tape/washi tape
- Low temp hot glue gun and glue (ages 5+ or at your discretion)
- Hammer and nails (ages 5+ or at your discretion)
- Wood scraps
- Fabric scraps

- Yarn
- Sewing needles and embroidery thread
- Scissors with patterns
- Stickers
- Paper punchers
- Ruler
- Brayer and other printmaking supplies
- Paint roller
- Painting tools such as wacky brushes, combs, or plastic cards for scraping
- Plastic cars and animals for painting/using with playdough
- Beads and beading materials (stretchy cord is great for kids)
- Pipe cleaners
- Flexible wire
- Clay (air dry)
- Bleeding colored tissue paper
- Toothpicks
- Foil
- Coffee filters
- Clear contact paper
- Blank greeting cards
- Envelopes
- Framed canvases

- Recycling bin items (empty containers, boxes, cardboard scraps, plastic lids, bubble wrap, egg cartons, magazines, junk mail envelopes)
- Art resource books, such as books with project ideas or how to draw using step-by-step instructions (ages 7+)
- Clipboards with printouts (with blank story writing pages/comic strips)

Some "extra goody" drawing tools organized in a caddy.

YOUR ART SPACE IS NOT JUST FOR ART

Don't feel limited to putting only art supplies in this space. Think of it more as a workshop, where your child can use art materials to enhance other types of work. I like to include a few plastic toys in our art space (so they can be washed off if they get glue or paint on them). Other play items we have used include calculators, sales slips or restaurant receipts (from the office supply store), play kitchen tools, and wood blocks. When I taught toddler art classes, our toy cars and animals were often the most popular tools for painting and exploring the art materials. We sometimes keep little dolls in our playroom and my kids end up using the art supplies to make homes and accessories for them. Art-making becomes woven into their imaginative play, which can keep them engaged for long periods of time.

Having accessible art supplies makes it easy to create additional toys. The box in this photo has become a building for this toy man and his car.

This microscope and science book in a child's art space offer more ways to explore the natural world beyond the art supplies.

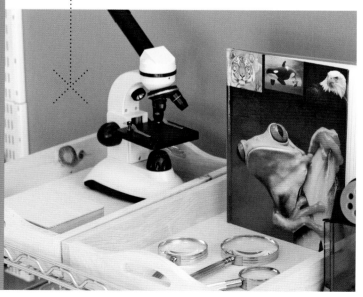

USING AN ART SPACE FOR TINKERING & INVENTING

BY RACHELLE DOORLEY OF TINKERLAB®

As my children have grown, our maker space has moved all over our home, from the kitchen counter to the dining table to a dedicated maker corner that now houses self-serve materials, musical instruments, and tinkering supplies. While I like to think of this space as a TinkerLab®, my kids simply call the table their "art table." And while it certainly hosts its fair share of painting parties, it's far more than that! When a new idea strikes, be it the invention of a new board game or a contraption to conserve water, my kids head to the art table and the making begins. Since most of the supplies they need are at their fingertips (e.g., recycled materials, paint, stapler, string, paper), there is very little friction between their idea and execution. And like inventors with a problem to solve, they chip away with their tools and supplies to come up with solutions and creations that didn't previously exist.

ADDING TINKERING AND MAKER MATERIALS INTO YOUR ART SPACE

Art spaces for kids are places of exploration, investigation, discovery, and creation. It's important not to limit your materials to only art supplies (especially for kids over age three), but to offer kids a variety of materials to enhance their learning experience.

Tinkering = To mess around with, to improve, to repair
Maker = Someone who constructs, builds, produces, invents, designs

A great way to offer kids the opportunity to tinker and make things is to have tinker trays on display (or have them ready to bring out when you want) and to have building materials and child-sized real tools. A tinker tray is simply a divided tray filled with small tinker materials. Tinker trays allow for organization and easy access to a variety of small loose parts that can be used when tinkering and making.

Kids go crazy for real tools! Just like using quality art supplies, children feel trusted when allowed to use real tools and—with a little guidance—they will treat them with respect. Child-sized real tools are easier to use and more effective than adult-sized tools or children's play tools. If your art space is not a good place to introduce certain tools (such as a hammer), maybe you can have them available outside, once in a while. Think about what tools you're comfortable with in your art space and start with that.

Ideas for Small Items to Put in Tinker Trays

- Beads
- Toothpicks
- Washers
- Nuts
- Bolts
- Paper clips
- Brads
- Pebbles
- Old keys
- Key rings
- Wire
- Pipe cleaners
- Rubber bands
- Shells
- Bottle caps
- Golf tees
- Googly eyes
- Gems
- Buttons
- Clothes pins
- Straws
- Small wood pieces/shapes
- Corks
- Popsicle sticks
- Screws and nails (if you have a screwdriver and hammer)

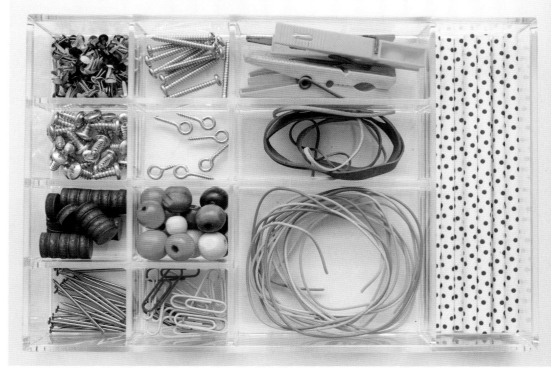

Tinker tray.

Ideas for Larger Tinker Items and Maker Tools to Have in Your Art Space

- Tinfoil
- Tape measure
- Safety glasses
- Scissors
- Low temp hot glue gun
- Glue sticks for glue gun
- Duct tape
- Masking tape
- Items from your recycle bin (cardboard tubes, egg cartons, plastic packaging, etc.)
- Fabric scraps
- Magnets
- Old electronic items to dismantle
- Screwdriver
- Hammer
- Balsa wood blocks (balsa wood is very soft and easy to hammer into)
- Sand paper
- LEGO/building toys
- Graph paper
- Tracing paper
- Tweezers
- Magnifying glass

Kids can learn how to use real tools like a hammer and nail while working in their art space.

PLANNING YOUR ART SPACE

Now that you have an idea of what art supplies you will put in your space, you can begin to plan the layout and storage options. First choose some areas in your home that are possible locations for your art space. If you are using your kitchen or dining table as a creative surface, try to find a spot for the art supplies nearby. If not, remember that young kids like to be near their parents/caregivers. If you choose a basement or a spot in an out-of-the-way guest room, be prepared to be in the art space with your child while she works. If you have a toddler, you will most likely have to be with him around art supplies anyway, but as he learns how to use the materials and the space safely, you will eventually want to let him wander over unaccompanied. If you want to add an art space to a remote playroom or if you have an extra room for a full-size art playroom, you can keep a portable caddy available for using in other areas of the house.

Photo Credit: Catalina Gutierrez

CHOOSING A LOCATION

BY JEAN VAN'T HUL OF THE ARTFUL PARENT

Sometimes when we decide to set up an art space for our children, we choose any currently unused space in the house. I think that's a mistake. Often that space is the least desirable and is unused for a reason. If you are setting up an art space for your kids, you're doing it because you want to encourage their art and creativity, right? You want to show them that you value creativity in general and their creativity specifically. You are going to spend a certain amount of time, effort, and expense to set up an art space, and you want it to be used. So don't choose the cast-off, unwanted space in the house. Choose the best space. That's right. Choose the space where everyone gravitates already—the kitchen table, the corner spot by the living room window . . . and find a way to make it an art space as well.

You can have a mini art space wherever you go with this portable art box.

Photo Credit: Fynn Sor

FURNITURE, STORAGE, AND TIPS ON ORGANIZING ART SUPPLIES FOR DIFFERENT AGES

Gathering Ideas

When you start to gather ideas for your art space, make sure to keep a collection of these ideas for easy reference. I like to create a dedicated Pinterest board for each project to keep track of inspiration and possible products to purchase. Alternatively, you can collect your ideas and product information in a word document, spreadsheet, or even in a written notebook. You will want to record the product name and place to purchase (ideally with a link), the price, the measurements, the quantity you will need, and any other relevant notes.

DESIGN TIP

Things to consider: Does the space have natural light? Is there adequate overhead lighting? Do you need to add task lighting? Choose a spot with lots of natural light if you can.

MEASURING TIP

Make sure to take measurements of your space before you begin looking for furniture and containers. Always measure the length, depth, and height of your space, of each wall that you will use for storage, and of any other sections or furniture that you will be including in your art area. I always keep a small tape measure in my purse for in-store purchases. That way, I'll never bring home a piece of furniture that is too large for the space or a container that doesn't fit on the shelf.

RESEARCH TIP

When you jot down or save a product, remember to include the dimensions and price in your description, for quick reference.

Lessons from Families

I have had several clients who wanted to create an art space in their playrooms, which were located in extra rooms away from the central action of the house. When I asked if the kids ever play in their playrooms, many of them replied no and admitted that the kids like to play near them. So we found new locations for the art spaces that were tucked away in their family spaces, where the kids like to be. This means that the art spaces end up being smaller than the alternative, but they actually get used!

The Layout

Sketch out basic shapes to create the layout for the space plan. Generally, the table will be either in the middle of the space or against a wall. If you have room, it's ideal to have the table in the middle of the space so kids can move freely around their work surface.

Drawing out the basic shapes of the furniture (roughly to scale) in your art space allows you to see how it might all fit together.

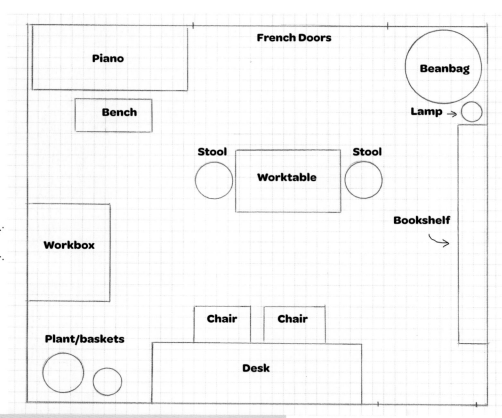

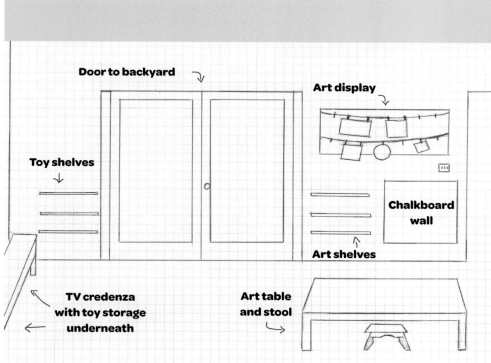

Sketching the items that will be placed against a wall of your art space will help you in your planning.

Think about the wall space. Where would a good spot be for accessing supplies? Ideally, you would find some wall space for low shelving and containers so that your child can access some supplies on his own. You will probably also want some supplies stored out of reach so that you can be in control of when and how these supplies are used. If you have open shelving (and open or clear containers), kids can see these out-of-reach supplies and therefore will ask to use them more often. If you don't want your child to see these out-of-reach supplies, then you will need either closed cabinets or shelving with containers that hide the supplies. As you think about the space, decide where your table and storage will go, then begin your search for the right ones.

Table and Chairs

Start with a table. The table will most likely be the largest, most prominent item in the space, so it will set the mood for the rest of the furniture. Many families use their dining tables as their creative surface, which works well, but requires constant cleanup. If you have extra space, a dedicated child-sized table allows for kids to pause their work and come back to it over multiple sessions. You can find or make tables in all kinds of styles and sizes. Think about the decor style of your home and start searching for tables that will reflect this style.

Pay attention to the height of the table and chairs. When children are sitting down, the ideal table height for art is right around mid-belly. Standard tables are usually a little higher, but if you make your own it's good to think about. This is also why, as kids get older, art playrooms often have stools to position them higher.

DESIGN TIP

If you have access to a miter saw or table saw, you can cut the legs down from an adult-sized table to a child-sized table. This works well with simple wooden table legs (like the INGO table from Ikea).

This is an example of the table being at mid-belly for a child.

Standard Sizes for Pairing Tables and Chairs

- 23"–24" (58.5–61 cm) high table with 14" (35.5 cm) seat-height chairs for ages 3–6.

- 17"–18" (43–45.5 cm) high table with 11"–12" (28–30 cm) seat-height chairs for toddlers.

- Ideal size if you are making your own table: 20"–23" (50.5–58.5 cm) table with 14"–16" (35.5–40.5 cm) seat height chairs (table at mid-belly) for ages 3–6.

MAKE YOUR OWN TABLE

You can customize the size of your table for much less than the price of purchasing a ready-made table!

- Get a simple piece of wood/desktop and table legs at around 18"–22" (45.5–56 cm) high, depending on your chairs and child's age.

- 18"–19" (45.5–48 cm) legs are great for chairs with 12" (30 cm) seat height

- 20"–22" (50.5–56 cm) legs are great for chairs with 14" (35.5 cm) seat height

- Attach the legs with recommended hardware (usually with a power drill and screws) to the bottom of the tabletop.

It's that easy!

What *Not* to Do

I was once attending an art class with my then 18-month-old daughter. All of the kids in the class were between 18 months and 2 years, but the table height was made for kids ages 3 and over. These small toddlers were sitting on low chairs and had to reach upwards to do their work. I grimaced as they struggled to gain control over their supplies with no luck. Pretend for a moment that you are sitting in a chair and the table height is at your shoulders. Imagine trying to do anything in this position!

There are many inexpensive toddler-sized table and chair sets offered by various home-furnishing stores. These tables have small surfaces and are perfect for toddlers or single children, but I don't recommend them for an art space for multiple kids unless you push two of these tables together. When doing art, kids should have room to move their arms around without knocking elbows with someone else. It's also important to have enough space for a tray or large piece of paper. A decent sized table is often worth the investment. For more than one child, I would recommend a table no smaller than 23" (58.5 cm) wide by 40" (101.5 cm) long.

Another splurge that pays off over time is an adjustable-height table. These tables usually adjust from toddler-height to child-sized. Some even go up to adult-sized (which can be turned into a desk when your child is old enough). These are often more expensive than fixed height tables, but will last a long time.

Storage

Once you have decided on your art supplies and your space plan, taken measurements of the space, and chosen your table, it's time to start searching for your storage items. You will want to find either shelving or a storage unit that will complement your home decor style and function well in this space.

I almost always use open shelving in my designs. This is a great way to have easy access to supplies, with low and high access points. You can opt for a stand-alone unit (like a bookshelf) or you can install wall shelves (that are held up by brackets or attached to a bracket system on your wall). A stand-alone unit is often easier to put together than installing wall shelves and is more mobile. On the other hand, wall shelves can be customized to different heights and lengths. Closed storage, like cabinets, closets, armoires, or drawer units are good options for concealing supplies in multi-functional rooms. If your art space is located in your living room or kitchen, you may not want to have your supplies visible all the time.

The common phrase, "Out of sight, out of mind," is often true with kids and art supplies. If you have to store supplies in a closed cabinet, try to leave it open once in a while to remind your child of its existence. You can also put out Invitations to Create that will jump-start the creative process and will most likely lead your child over to the art cabinet to gather more supplies (see Part 2: Invitations to Create).

An example of wall-mounted, open shelving.

DESIGN TIP
Wall shelves can make your space feel larger because you have an uninterrupted sightline along the floor.

The shelving in the background is an example of a low bookshelf with adjustable shelves.

ADDITIONAL OPTIONS FOR STORING ART SUPPLIES

Wall organizers

Rolling cart

Desk top organizers:
Tiered fruit stand, caddy, baskets, buckets, jars, lazy Susan divided container, spice rack, mini drawers

An example of a wall organizer.

DESIGN TIP
If you are storing items in an armoire or cabinet, use a lazy Susan for hard-to-reach shelves and corners.

An example of a rolling cart.

A different type of wall organizer. This one has magnetic cups that can be removed and placed on a table when in use.

MEASURING TIP
Keep in mind the depth of the shelving or unit. You will probably want it to be at least 10" (25.5 cm) deep, which is enough to hold a paper organizer for basic 9" × 12" (22.5 × 30 cm) paper.

Desktop organizers can be as simple as this caddy.

CONTAINERS

Finding the right containers for your storage furniture and your supplies is probably the hardest part of setting up an art space. Here are a few of my favorite ways to choose containers for a space:

PRODUCT TIP
While shopping for art supply containers, make sure to check out the kitchen section of a store. Kitchen containers tend to be perfect for art supplies!

Collected Look:

You can use random containers that you have on hand, for example, unused baskets, bins, and other vessels lying around the house. This creates a lived-in, collected feel. You can get a similar look by finding containers at garage sales or thrift stores, giving the space a vintage vibe. These options are inexpensive, but can sometimes appear messy because your eye is bouncing around to look at the variety of textures, colors, and sizes of containers.

Streamlined Modern Look:

Find containers that have simple lines and are similar in color and style. When you use neutral colors or translucent containers, the art supplies become the stars of the space.

Streamlined Natural Look:

For a natural look, you can still have it feel streamlined by finding containers that are in a similar natural material (e.g., all medium brown woven and wood containers). These, too, will allow the art supplies to stand out, while giving the space a warm feeling.

Mixed Contemporary Look:

This look is a combination of modern and natural with some added pops of colored containers. The key here is sticking with a simple color scheme and balance. If you do purchase a mix of colored containers, try to keep a balance between neutral, natural, and color. I like to choose one or two pops of color and add a few pieces in these colors. Then I bring these colors into the rest of the space in the furniture or other items.

DESIGN TIP
When you have decided on your furniture and containers, you can create a mood board to see how the products and colors go together. A mood board is simply a collage of some of the main items that will be in your space.

Easels

To easel or not to easel? Having an easel in your art space isn't essential, but they do provide a unique opportunity for vertical painting and drawing. Standing easels help with children's gross motor development as well. There are a lot of children's easels on the market, so whether you need an easel that is inexpensive, adjustable, or wall mounted, you will most likely find one to fit your needs.

Make Your Own Wall Easel (That Doubles as a Printing Surface)

- Decide on the size you want for the painting surface.
- Order a piece of acrylic (plexiglass) cut to size from a plastics shop.
- Drill the acrylic panel into the wall.
- Drill art clips into the top of the panel.
- Install a shallow shelf underneath the panel for holding paint cups (or position a side table next to the easel to hold supplies).

Children's Easel Options

- One-sided: Good for one child
- Double-sided: Good for siblings
- Wall easel: Good for saving space
- Table easel: Mobile and good for saving space
- Double-sided transparent easel: Good for siblings and printmaking
- Adjustable easel: Good for lasting many years
- Toddler-height easel: Good for young children

This is a wall-mounted acrylic board that can be used as an easel or painted on directly.

SETTING UP AN ART SPACE FOR OLDER CHILDREN (AGES 8+)

If you are setting up an art space for an older child, there are a few key differences to note. When deciding on containers, older children aren't as overwhelmed as young children by the number of supplies visible. While baskets are wonderful for young children to keep things feeling soothing and minimal, clear containers work well for older kids. Clear, stackable containers are great space savers! Stackable containers are hard for young kids to access easily, but older kids can grab what they need with no problem.

With the addition of more tools as kids get older, I love to incorporate a tool board into an art space for older children. Tool boards can be found at home improvement stores or office supply stores. A wall-mounted display of tools makes the space feel even more like a workshop and keeps tools top of mind.

Older children can use a wider variety of tools and materials than young children. I have found that older kids love to make practical items that can be worn or used in their daily life. Adding materials for activities, such as beading, fabric decoration, sewing, woodworking, and tinker/maker materials, are all exciting additions to an art space for older children (you'll find these items in the previous lists for "Extra Goodies" and "Tinker/Maker" materials). You can also add art resource books with project ideas or books that teach kids a specific skill.

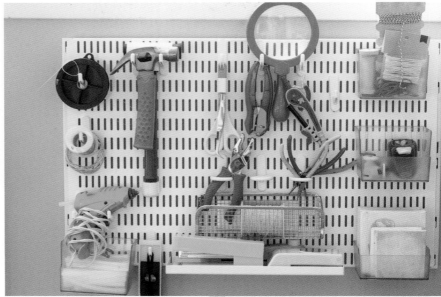

An example of a wall-mounted tool board.

For drying art, this art space uses a rack meant to organize kitchen pot lids. It also has a spot to display art with twine and clothespins.

ART STORAGE AND DISPLAY

When setting up your art space, don't forget to include areas for drying, storing, and displaying your child's art. If you have a little extra space, include a small drying rack or shelf. Otherwise, you may end up drying artwork on the floor or on your kitchen counter! We use a shoe rack as a drying rack. We also use a large paper tray for storing finished art when dry. When it fills up, we go through the artwork together and save our favorites. Depending on the size of your space, you can have an art display area as small as a picture frame or as large as an entire wall.

This art space uses a board with twine and clothespins to display art.

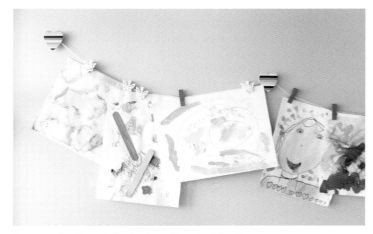

A Few Art Display Ideas
- Frame gallery wall
- Wire or twine line with clothespins
- Corkboard
- Magnet board or magnetic wall
- Empty wall for securing art with decorative craft tape
- Clips or clothespins attached to a piece of wood, then mounted to wall
- Keepsake frame (that easily opens to store multiple pieces of art)

An example of an art display line with colorful wall attachments and clothespins.

ADDING THE ART SUPPLIES

Once the table and storage area are ready to go, you can then set up the containers. I love the visual of an art space stocked with empty containers, just waiting to be filled with colorful, creative materials. Think about what supplies will go into each container and whether you want your child to access these supplies.

If your child is still in the dumping stage (supplies get dumped out of their containers and end up all over the floor), only put out very small portions of supplies at any given time. If there are eight markers in a container, rather than fifty, it will take a lot less time to clean them up. Put the rest of the supplies out of reach in organized, labeled bins so you can replenish or rotate items when necessary.

You can choose to do this part by yourself or include your child in deciding where to put the supplies. When children help with this step, they are more inclined to remember where everything is and they also feel more ownership of the space. This can be a great time to talk about the materials as you put them away with your child.

ORGANIZING TIP
Kids can get overwhelmed by too many choices and will probably end up using the same few items each time. Keep your art space organized by minimizing what supplies you have on display. Keep any extra supplies stored away and rotate them in whenever you want to rejuvenate your space.

Lessons from Families

I once had a client with a gorgeous art space in her playroom. When I first came to check it out, all of the supplies were hidden in a closet or tucked away on a high shelf. The space was left with completely bare shelving and looked sad and abandoned. The reason the supplies weren't accessible was because every time she put them out (each stacked with way too many markers, colored pencils, and crayons), her kids would dump them all out. She would end up spending an hour picking them up. So even though the design of the space was awesome, it didn't function well because of the way the supplies had been organized. I helped her pare down her accessible supplies so that even if everything were dumped out, cleanup wouldn't be too overwhelming. We moved any extra supplies into a storage area where she can now take out additional supplies when needed.

If you're not sure what to leave accessible and what to put out of reach, here is a suggested list for reference:

FOR LOWER SHELF

Supplies for Toddlers to Access Themselves

- Drawing paper
- Washable markers
- Washable crayons
- Toys (plastic cars, animals, etc.)
- Toddler-sized stamps and washable inkpads
- Plastic scissors that only cut paper
- Natural materials
- Fabric scraps

FOR MID-HEIGHT SHELF

Supplies for Children Ages 3+ to Access Themselves
Anything on the lower shelf list plus . . .

- Washable tempera paint (in nonspill paint cups with lids)
- Watercolor cake palettes
- Paint brushes
- Collage items
- Pipe cleaners
- Tape
- Glue sticks
- Playdough and tools
- Pencils
- Colored pencils
- Paint paper

FOR MID-HEIGHT OR HIGH SHELF

Depending on the Child

- Glue
- Scissors
- Glitter
- Clay
- Oil pastels (they are not washable)
- Chalk pastels (they are really dusty)
- Wire
- Duct tape

FOR HIGH SHELF

For Adult Supervision or Help Setting Up

- Acrylic paints (they are not washable)
- Sharpies/permanent markers
- Hot glue gun and glue
- Liquid watercolors (they can be messy to distribute in cups)

ORGANIZING TIP
Lose the packaging! No matter how cute a package might be, it's almost always better to let it go. Take supplies out of their packaging and store them in your easy-to-access containers. The exception would be for items that come in travel cases, or are necessary to protect the materials (like boxes for soft chalk pastels).

In this space, toddler art supplies are in the floor baskets and on the lowest shelf. Supplies for an older preschool-aged child are on the top shelf and additional supplies are in the closed cabinets above to use with parental guidance.

CHAPTER 3
Your Art Playroom Is Ready to Go, Now What?

Once your art space is organized and fully stocked, your child will be eager to get her hands on it. If you've got an experienced artist, she will most likely jump right in and start working with the familiar materials. If not, you'll have to spend some time introducing her to the materials (see the section ahead, Introducing Your Child to the Materials). But what happens after a few weeks? Will your child continually use the same few materials out of habit, leaving the rest untouched? Will the space begin to look disheveled and cluttered?

Remember how your art space is like your kitchen pantry? Well, in order to provide optimum nourishment, you need to keep ingredients visible and fresh and understand how to use them. Before you even get started, it's good to have a plan.

KEEPING MATERIALS VISIBLE AND FRESH

The best way to keep your art supplies visible is to keep the space organized and clutter-free. Of course, things will (and should) get messy during the creative process, but if you make a quick sweep of the space every two weeks or so, it will make a massive difference. Remove items that don't belong and put things back in their places.

It's important to keep your child involved in the organizing process, so he will eventually learn how to do this himself. When you first set up your art space, show your child where everything belongs or have him help with deciding where things go. During cleanup, you may need to remind him once or twice (or many times!) where everything goes.

Keep materials in good shape (toss dried out markers or broken tools—or better yet, find ways to repurpose them). Help your child learn to respect the tools and materials by showing him how to clean them and put them away without damaging them.

Introduce new materials once in a while. Put them out on the table for your child to investigate and test (see the next section, Introducing Your Child to the Materials). Then decide with your child on a good place to store them in the art space.

When you get new materials, rotate some old materials out and store them in another location (e.g., put them in a bin in a closet). When you feel the need to shake things up, bring back the ones in hiding and rotate out some of the others.

INTRODUCING YOUR CHILD TO THE MATERIALS

Now that you have a plan for keeping your art space organized, it's important that your child understands how to use the materials. It's much harder to cook when you don't know anything about your ingredients, right? What happens when you boil a vegetable vs. roast it? What ingredients taste great together? You can learn a lot about art supplies when you approach them with the same curiosity. Unlike food, you can't really go wrong when it comes to art exploration and your child will gain a deeper understanding of these materials when she discovers how they work on her own. So rather than instructing her how to use the materials, you can guide this exploratory process by asking probing questions.

They Really Will Get It

After about a year of reminding my two-year-old to put the caps back on the markers, she finally began to do it about 25 percent of the time. When she did remember, she would say, "Mommy, look, I put the top on!" and she would hold up her capped marker with a huge grin.

TESTING NEW MATERIALS

When you introduce new materials, encourage your child to test each medium to understand its unique qualities and uses. You can test things like how it creates lines, how it fills in shapes, or what it looks like on different surfaces (paper, cardboard, fabric, foil, plastic, etc.).

QUESTIONS TO ASK YOUR CHILD WHEN TESTING DIFFERENT MATERIALS

Drawing Tools
(such as crayons, colored pencils, oil pastels, markers, and chalk) Does it make a thin line or a thick line? Does it make a faint or bold mark on paper? Does it smear if rubbed? If so, what happens if you blend two colors together?

Watercolor Paints
Experiment with color mixing and application. What happens when you mix red and blue together? How does changing the amount of water change the way the paint looks or moves on the paper? What happens when you dab your painting with a towel? Can you move the paint around by tilting your paper?

Tempera Paint
Experiment with color mixing, brush types, and texture. What happens when you mix three colors together? How does this chubby brush make the paint look different from this fine brush? What happens when you add water or something textured, like sand, to the paint?

Glue and Collage Items
Set out different glues and small bits of paper or collage pieces (sequins, buttons, paper shapes, etc.) and have a few different types of surfaces to glue onto: thin paper, thick paper, cardboard, plastic, etc. Remind your child to check them when they are dry to see whether they stuck well to the surface or whether the surface was strong enough to hold all the glue.

Modeling Materials
(such as playdough or clay—explore separately) Set out your modeling material on the table with a few different modeling tools (one to poke it, one to roll it, and another to cut it). Sit with your child and investigate how you can use these tools with your material. Can you make a hole? Can you roll it into a ball? Can you cut it? Can you flatten it? Can you make it stand up tall?

Wire/Pipe Cleaners
First wrap the ends of wire with masking tape so they aren't sharp. Invite your child to bend them, coil them around a pencil or stick, and wrap them together. Can you make an object out of wire? Can you add beads to the wire?

Mixed Media and Techniques
Once you have tested your materials separately, you can set up explorations to see how the materials interact with each other. These activities can be done completely randomly, led by your child (see which materials your child wants to combine and wing it), or you can strategically teach techniques by exploring together and modeling the technique for your child.

They Really Will Get It

When I was an art teacher, I never told the kids how much glue to use. The parents thought I was crazy! The glue would pool up and ooze over the paper, sometimes filling the art trays to the brim. I would say, "Go ahead and squeeze as much as you want. Let's see what happens." Later on, we would check the artwork. Did the glue dry well? Did it hold the materials to the paper? Did the paper hold up under all that glue? Then one day we did a collage project and my students (still toddlers) carefully squeezed out small amounts of glue and placed the materials nicely on each glue dot. They had self-regulated and discovered on their own how the materials worked best. I was a proud teacher that day!

PART 2

INVITATIONS TO

CREATE

CHAPTER 4

Keeping Your Child Engaged Over Time with *Invitations to Create*

When your art space is inviting and organized with visible, fresh materials, your child will continue to use this space. But after a while, you may find that she is only minimally engaging with her art supplies, or she is stuck in the habit of using the same few materials again and again. Our art space is stocked with all sorts of fun items, yet when my older daughter was five years old, she got into the habit of choosing the same basic markers each time she wanted to make something. Every day, she would draw the same thing: an anime-type character with a large head and big eyes. Markers happened to be her medium of choice and I supported that. But I also wanted to challenge her and encourage her to experiment with materials that were out of her comfort zone. If you find yourself in the same boat or if you just want to bring back excitement into your art space, try setting up *Invitations to Create*. Over time, this simple exercise can be a real game-changer.

WHAT ARE INVITATIONS TO CREATE?

Imagine your child walking into a room to discover a few art materials thoughtfully arranged on the table.

This curious display is fresh and intriguing, inviting him to sit down and engage. This is an *Invitation to Create*, sometimes called a prompt or provocation. I like to describe them as **open-ended art prompts**. They often involve a novel or surprising component that sparks curiosity and entices kids to explore the materials. Invitations are a great way to deepen your child's art experience and encourage new ways of using familiar materials.

Setting up an *Invitation to Create* is easy. It should be done while your child is out of the room so that she can discover it on her own. I like to set up invitations while my kids are asleep so they can work on them in the morning. Another great time to set up an invitation is while your child is at school. It can be a calming afternoon activity, perfect for a little down time.

It's This Easy

Take a few minutes to arrange some materials on your creative surface (art table, kitchen table, tray, etc.). The materials can range from simple to complex and can be familiar or completely new items. Display them in an interesting way that looks purposeful and inviting. Only use a few different materials each time. Presenting the materials in an interesting way will spark your child's curiosity and beckon him to play.

Imagine how special your child will feel to have a thoughtfully prepared surprise waiting for him each day!

10 TIPS ON SETTING UP INVITATIONS TO CREATE

1) For the first invitation, put out something that is familiar to your child, but add a new twist. The key for this first time is that your child is confident with the materials, but pushed to explore them in a new way.

2) If your child doesn't notice this setup, you can casually mention that there is something interesting on the table. If your child often resists your suggestions, it is best to let her discover this prompt on her own.

3) Be consistent. Try to put out something (even if it's only two items), every day until you notice a change. Challenge yourself to do this for a week and see what happens. How does it affect your child's relationship to the materials?

4) Rotate between simple invitations (Peekaboo Drawing, page 59) and more complex/involved invitations (Eye-Catching Eruption, page 115), depending on your energy and time.

5) With each new invitation, you can get more creative in your selection. Your child will catch on and look forward to the challenge.

6) Try not to have an outcome in mind. Let your child use the materials in his own way (as long as he follows your house rules). If you want to help your child expand his thinking, you can ask questions that might provoke new ways of using the materials.

7) An invitation isn't a challenge to only use those specific materials (though if your child wants to make it a challenge, that's awesome!) So don't be discouraged if she decides to add different materials to the mix. The goal is to engage and inspire!

8) An invitation can be something your child does alone, with siblings, or with friends. Or it can be something you and your child do together, bouncing ideas off each other, exploring the materials together with wonder.

9) Trays are your friend! Use a large plastic tray or cookie sheet when painting, gluing, or using playdough to make cleanup easier. Trays are also great if you want to set up the project ahead of time, but don't want to leave it on the table. Just move the tray and plop it on the table when you're ready.

10) Remember, have it set up in advance so your child can stumble upon the intriguing arrangement of materials!

"Every morning, after breakfast, my girls now check out what art supplies I laid out for them the night before. It gives me enough time to wash dishes, make lunches, and prep dinner. I much prefer my mornings like these instead of hearing TV in the background." —Jonalyn J.

CHAPTER 5
Starter *Invitations* to Create

Easy art prompts for ages two to seven that are quick to set up and easy for young children to explore on their own

These starter art prompts are meant to be simple *Invitations to Create,* with no intended outcome. I have chosen most of these materials because they need no explanation and can be explored in a variety of ways (although younger children may need your help to facilitate the exploration). These are just suggestions, feel free to come up with your own ideas, mix and match, or substitute materials based on what you have at home.

EASY ART PROMPTS

(Ages 2–7)

MONOCHROMATIC SHAPE

Kids are so used to drawing on rectangular paper that simply changing the shape of the paper will spark curiosity in your child. You can set out a circle, a triangle, an octagon, or even a wavy blob—whatever shape is easy for you to cut out! You can try this on several different occasions with various shapes and see how the drawings change based on the shape of the paper. The combination of this paper shape and monochromatic drawing tools brings new interest to a basic drawing experience. This prompt also helps kids understand how one color can look different, depending on which tool is used.

MATERIALS

- **Piece of paper cut into an interesting shape**
- **Various drawing tools (marker, crayon, colored pencil, etc.) in the same color**

SETUP

Line up the monochromatic drawing tools next to the paper shape on your art table so that it looks thoughtfully placed. This sends a signal to your child that you took time and care to prepare this invitation.

TIP
To get a perfect circle, try tracing the rim of a bowl.

FOIL PAINTING

This simple prompt introduces a novel (and shiny!) painting surface to get your child's creative juices flowing.

MATERIALS

- Aluminum foil
- A few colors of tempera paint (poster paint) on a paint tray or plate
- Paintbrush
- Cotton swabs
- Cup of water and rag for washing the paintbrush (optional)

SETUP

Place a piece of foil on your table/tray and tape the corners down with masking tape. Place the paint tray and paintbrush next to the foil. Place one cotton swab in each color of paint.

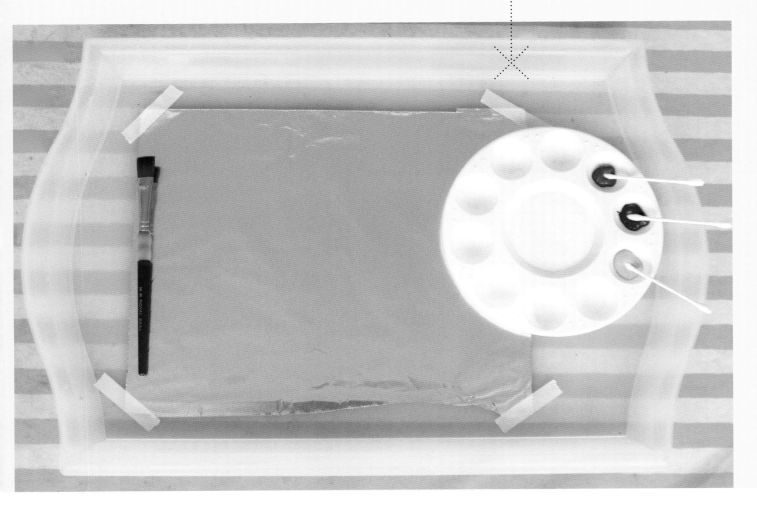

PLAYDOUGH SCULPTURE

Playdough is a fun and easy material for kids to explore. This particular prompt offers a new way of combining playdough with sculptural materials. Your child may poke the playdough with the toothpicks or she may stick them all into the one large ball of playdough like a porcupine. The smaller balls may spark the idea to connect pieces of playdough with the toothpicks. The beads and buttons slide easily onto the toothpicks so your child may discover that he can thread the toothpicks with colorful decoration, or he may just push the beads and buttons deep into the playdough. See what he comes up with!

TIP
If you want to encourage building with the toothpicks, you can include an example of a few toothpicks connected with small balls of playdough to show how this works.

MATERIALS

- Playdough
- Toothpicks
- Beads/buttons

SETUP

Roll a piece of playdough into a ball. Roll a few smaller pieces of playdough into small balls. Arrange on a tray with toothpicks and an assortment of beads and buttons.

CRAFT TAPE CONSTRUCTION

Kids love tape and colorful craft tape is even better! This prompt is a fun way for kids to explore using tape with a variety of items from your junk bin or from nature.

MATERIALS

- Craft tape (but if you only have Scotch tape or plain masking tape, that works too!)
- Scissors
- Items from your recycle bin (toilet paper roll, plastic lids, containers, pieces of cardboard, corks, etc.)
- Sticks, twigs, or other items from nature

SETUP

Place the tape, scissors, and other items onto the table in an inviting way.

TIP
For toddlers, precut pieces of tape and stick them to the edge of the table or the rim of a bowl for easy access.

PEEKABOO DRAWING

This is a simple drawing prompt, but the novelty of the cut-out makes it more interesting than a basic piece of paper. The cut-out shape in the middle may also spark an idea of what to draw. It may become a window, a robot body, or even inspire a design of lines or rectangles in the surrounding area.

MATERIALS

- **Large paper with cut-out shape (rectangle, circle, triangle, etc.)**
- **Markers or crayons**

SETUP

To cut out a shape, fold the paper in half and cut half of the shape in the middle of paper, along the fold. Then unfold the paper. Place on the table alongside markers or crayons.

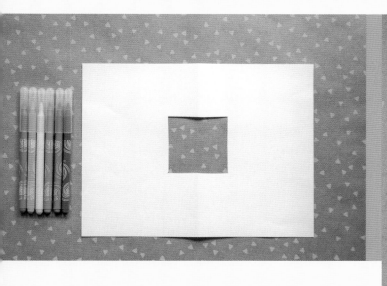

ROCK PAINTING

Kids love painting 3D objects and rock painting is especially fun when using smooth rocks. If the rocks are small, this can become practice for detailed painting.

MATERIALS

- Variety of smooth rocks
- A few colors of tempera paint (poster paint) on a paint tray or plate (for older kids, try acrylic paint which is permanent and will last longer outside)
- Fine paintbrush
- Cup of water and rag

SETUP

Place the rocks, paint, paintbrush, cup of water, and rag on a tray.

EXTEND & ENRICH
Try using paint pens instead of paint and a brush. This allows for very detailed work on a rock.

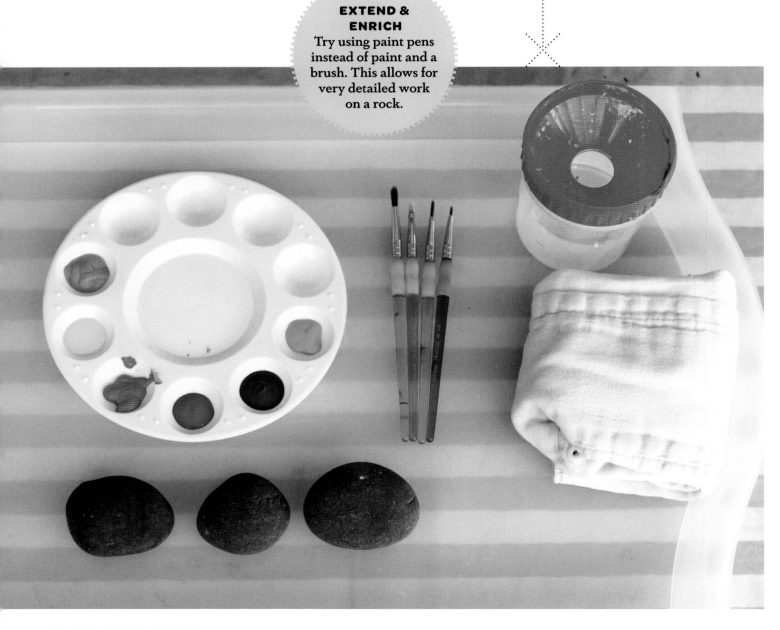

DOT PAINTING

Dot painting is an example of how you can make your own paintbrush with things you have around the house. Kids love painting with unexpected items! This prompt includes the three primary colors so it can also be a lesson in color mixing.

MATERIALS

- 3 cotton balls or pom-poms
- 3 clothespins
- Tempera paint (poster paint) in primary colors (red, yellow, and blue) on a tray/plate
- Paint paper

SETUP

Clip one cotton ball to the end of each clothespin. Place the clothespins, paint, and paper on a tray.

EXTEND & ENRICH
Try making paintbrushes out of other materials you find around the house. You can also use items from your art space or natural materials from outside!

PRODUCE PRINTS

Using produce to make prints is easy and fun. When cut in half, certain fruits and veggies make great shapes for printing.

EXTEND & ENRICH

If you want to sit with your child for this prompt, you can include a foam roller and show your child how to roll the roller through the paint and onto the flat side of the fruit/veggie before printing.

MATERIALS

- A few fruits or veggies (try an apple, potato, cremini mushroom, bell pepper, pear, or lemon)
- Tempera paint (poster paint) on a flat tray or plate
- Paper

SETUP

Cut the fruit/veggies in half (from the top to the bottom for the mushroom or pear, but from side to side for the others). Place the paper and plate of paint on a tray and lay one half of each fruit/veggie next to the paint or directly onto the paint.

DREAMY DECOUPAGE

Decoupage is a technique similar to collage, that involves gluing decorative bits of paper onto a surface. This prompt is a great way to introduce decoupage and always turns out colorful and sparkly (with the addition of glitter).

MATERIALS

- Heavy/thick paper (for the base)
- White school glue (or Mod Podge)
- Paintbrush (chubby or foam)
- Colored tissue paper
- Glitter

SETUP

Mix a small amount of glue with water (1:1 ratio) in a cup. Cut or rip tissue paper into small pieces. Place the base paper, the tissue paper, the cup of watered-down glue, the paintbrush, and the glitter side by side on a tray.

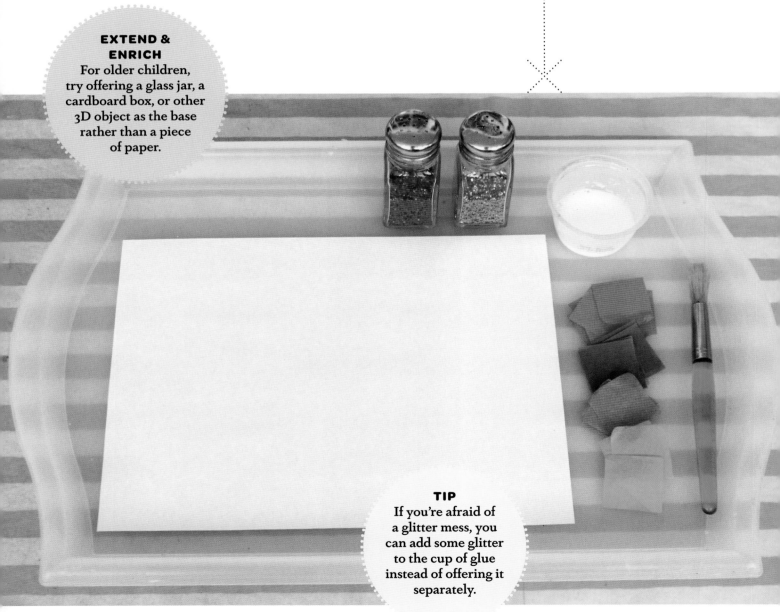

EXTEND & ENRICH
For older children, try offering a glass jar, a cardboard box, or other 3D object as the base rather than a piece of paper.

TIP
If you're afraid of a glitter mess, you can add some glitter to the cup of glue instead of offering it separately.

GRID DRAWING

Drawing on graph/grid paper is a new way for kids to draw and may spark something completely out of the ordinary in your child.

MATERIALS

- **Graph/grid paper**
- **Colored pencils and/or fine markers**

SETUP

You can use store-bought graph paper (with any size grid) or you can easily make your own by drawing a grid onto paper using a ruler. Place this grid paper next to the drawing tools.

EXTEND & ENRICH

Try this a few times using different sized grids. See if your child makes different choices based on the size of the squares in the grid.

SCRAPE-AND-ROLL PAINTING

Scrape-and-roll painting is another fun way to use unexpected items as a paintbrush. Paint moves differently when scraped across the paper using a flat edge (or when rolled across the paper using a round object) than it does with a standard paintbrush. This is a great way for kids to explore the qualities of paint and the many tools we can use for painting.

MATERIALS

- **Large paper or cardboard**
- **Tempera paint (poster paint) in squeeze bottles or cups**
- **Spoon for each cup of paint**
- **Rolling items (rolling pin, golf ball, marble for older kids)**
- **Scraping items (old plastic cards, squeegee, plastic putty knife, plastic fork, comb, etc.)**

SETUP

Place the paper/cardboard on a tray alongside the paint and tools. If needed, place a spoon in each cup of paint (for transferring the paint to the paper).

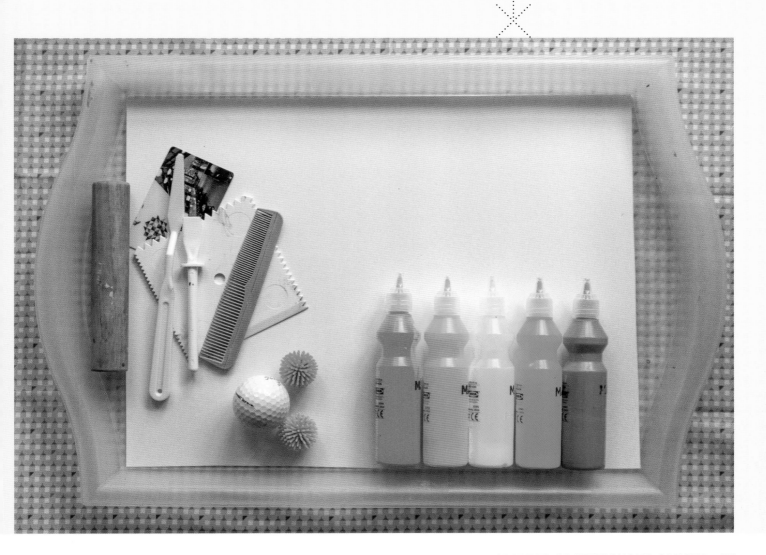

FINE FEATHERED FABRICATION

This is a simple construction prompt and can be enjoyed with a variety of scrap materials you have on hand. Kids love the process of taping and building, and may make something representative of a feathered creature or they may make an abstract sculpture. See what your child comes up with!

MATERIALS

- Feathers
- Leaves
- Tape (craft tape, Scotch tape, or masking tape)
- Toilet paper roll or cardboard box
- Any other scrap/recycled item
- Scissors

SETUP

Place the materials alongside each other in a purposeful and inviting way.

DIY STICKERS

Blank stickers offer two creative activities in one. Your child can first decorate the stickers and then use them in another art project right after or save them for a future project.

MATERIALS

- **Blank labels (from an office supply store) in any shape**
- **Fine markers**
- **Colored construction paper**

SETUP

Place the blank stickers, markers, and paper alongside each other on your table.

TIP
If you think your child might not know what the blank stickers are, you can make a sign that says, "Design your own stickers!" and place it in front of the materials.

STICKY BLOCK BUILDING

Using playdough with block building offers a unique way to connect blocks together. The playdough can hold pieces together that otherwise wouldn't stay connected (like when leaning a flat block against a taller block to make a slide). With this prompt, kids can build just for the sake of construction, or they can simultaneously add toy people, animals, or cars and engage in imaginative play while building.

- **Playdough**
- **Wood blocks/wood scraps**

Place the blocks on the table in an inviting way alongside some balls of playdough. You can create a provocation by connecting two blocks together using the playdough. The dough can be easily wiped off the wood blocks when finished.

EXTEND & ENRICH
Try including other building materials like popsicle sticks, toothpicks, items from your recycle bin, etc.

MISPLACED MURAL

Kids are used to working on the surface of a table so anything outside of that can be a fun surprise. This is a simple drawing prompt, but the large scale of the paper and the unexpected location makes it extra intriguing.

MATERIALS

- **Large paper cut from a roll of easel paper or butcher paper**
- **Drawing tools like markers or crayons**

SETUP

Tape the paper to a surprising location like a wall, a floor, or the underside of a table. Place the drawing tools in a container near the paper.

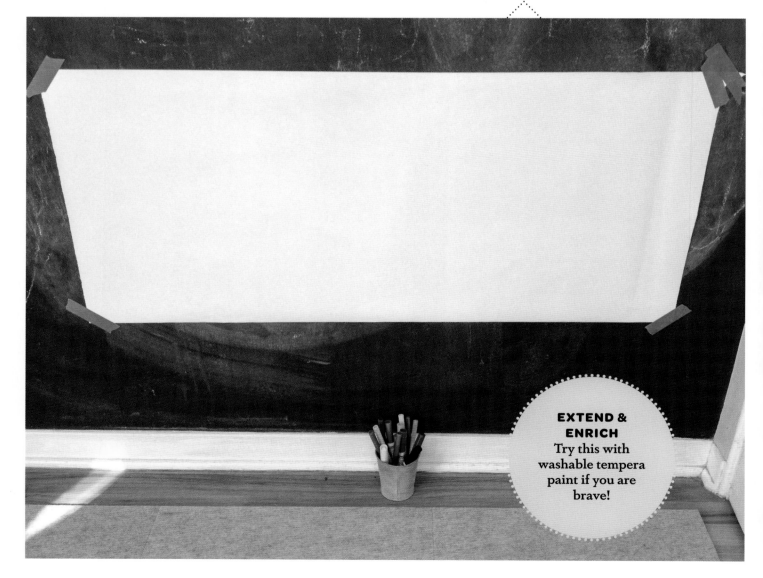

EXTEND & ENRICH
Try this with washable tempera paint if you are brave!

WET CHALK DRAWING

Chalk is an interesting drawing tool that swiftly changes consistency when wet. By providing a bowl of water with chalk, you are inviting your child to discover this first hand.

MATERIALS

- **Chalk**
- **Shallow bowl of water**
- **Black construction paper (or other dark paper)**

SETUP

Place the paper, chalk, and water on a tray.

EXTEND & ENRICH
Try this with large sidewalk chalk, a cheese grater, water, and a paintbrush. Grating the chalk will create powdered pigment that can turn into paint with the water and brush.

YOU'VE GOT MAIL

This prompt is a playful way to practice writing or prewriting skills. Kids love to write letters and stuff envelopes. It can easily flow into imaginative play with friends or siblings.

MATERIALS

- Envelopes
- Paper
- Scissors (optional)
- Fine markers
- Rubber stamp(s)
- Stamp pad

SETUP

Display the envelopes, rubber stamp, and stamp pad alongside the paper and markers on a table.

EXTEND & ENRICH
Make a mailbox (out of a cardboard box) so kids can drop their mail in when finished.

MIRROR, MIRROR

A mirror can be an interesting surface to paint, with its smooth glass and reflective qualities. This prompt may inspire kids to paint the reflection of their face in the mirror, or they may just paint something random on the glass. See what your child comes up with!

MATERIALS

- Mirror (a hand-held mirror or one that can stand up on the table)
- Tempera paint (poster paint) in a few colors on a tray/plate
- Paintbrushes

SETUP

Place the mirror, paint, and brushes alongside each other on a tray.

EXTEND & ENRICH

This same idea can also be explored at a large mirror on the wall (but it poses more of a risk of getting paint on your wall!). Alternatively, you can prop a large, framed mirror onto an easel.

"DO IT TOGETHER" STARTER INVITATIONS TO CREATE

(Ages 2–7)

These next few art prompts are best for children to explore with an adult. They introduce a new material or technique and can act as a simple art lesson. After first exploring together, you can set up these same prompts at another time and your child will be ready to explore on his own. The best way to explore materials together is to each have your own setup of materials. That way, you can model a technique on your own work, without interfering with your child's work (see the section on Testing New Materials on page 45).

OIL PASTELS AND OIL

Discover how oil pastels can turn into paint by simply adding a little oil! Your child likely won't need much direction with this.

Do It Together

Start by drawing with the pastels on your own paper, and then begin to explore with the oil and cotton swabs. Rather than explaining what to do, you can model your own investigation by saying something like, "I wonder what will happen if I dip this cotton swab into the oil and move it over the pastels?"

MATERIALS
- Oil pastels
- Small cup of oil (baby oil or vegetable oil)
- Cotton swabs
- Paint paper

SETUP

Place the paper, oil pastels, oil, and cotton swabs alongside each other on a tray.

CURRENT OBSESSION STILL LIFE

A still life drawing is an observational drawing of an inanimate object. The purpose of an observational drawing is to look closely at the shapes and lines of an object and draw what you see. This prompt offers a lesson in observational drawing with an object that is exciting to your child. Pick something that your child is currently obsessed with (a toy or other item) as the subject of this still life.

MATERIALS

- Child's toy or item of interest (something with simple lines or a simple shape is best)
- Black permanent marker
- Paint paper
- Watercolor paint
- Paintbrush
- Cup of water (for rinsing the paintbrush)
- Rag

SETUP

Place the object on a table with the paper, marker, and paint in front of the object.

Do It Together

Look at the object with your child. Talk about the shapes and lines that you see and ask what shapes and lines your child sees. Invite your child to draw the lines of the object with the permanent marker. After drawing, invite your child to color in the object with the watercolor paint. As long as the paint is watery and not too thick or opaque, your child can paint directly over the lines and they will still show through the paint.

COLOR MIXING

Understanding color mixing is an important artistic skill, but it's also a really fun activity. Kids love stirring paint and seeing two colors swirl into each other to create a new color!

Do It Together

Sit with your child and explore color mixing together. You can have your own setup if you have an extra paint tray. You can start by explaining that red, blue, and yellow are primary colors, which means that you can make most other colors using various combinations of these colors. Say something like, "I wonder what color I will make if I mix the red and the blue together?" As you mix them together you can say, "Wow, that makes purple! What happens if I put a little white into it?"

Adding white to a color will create a new "tint" of that color. Adding black to a color will create a new "shade" of that color. You can try adding black during this exploration, but I recommend waiting until a child is older or has some experience with color mixing before introducing black. Black can quickly overpower the other colors, so use it sparingly.

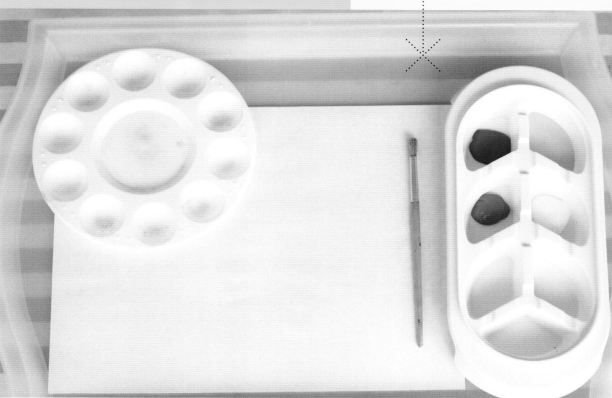

CHAPTER 6

Skill-Building
Invitations to Create

Art prompts to develop skills for ages two to ten

To get you thinking about how to encourage skill-building in your art space, I am including a variety of ideas for *Invitations to Create,* with an emphasis on specific skills. They are meant to be simple prompts that help children develop a particular skill. Kids learn through play and continual exposure to materials, which is why these playful art prompts are a great way to build skills. There is no intended outcome, just a hope that your child will explore the materials with curiosity.

Young children might need your help to facilitate the exploration, but try to let them explore in their own way as much as possible. Sometimes it can be helpful to include an example of what is possible with the materials in the invitation. You'll see this in the modeling clay invitation (in the Toy section). This is not to offer a prescribed outcome, but simply to spark your child's imagination, which seems to work better for older kids. If you think setting out an example will stifle your child's creativity, then first try it without the example.

MASTERING TOOLS

(Ages 3–8, or 2+ where noted)

Art prompts that encourage the use of creative tools

When your child is learning how to use specific tools (like scissors, a stapler, etc.), it's important to offer many opportunities to use these tools in the form of play and exploration. This type of practice is fun and intrinsically motivating, which will help your child master these tools with joy and confidence.

If this is your child's first experience using one of these tools, make sure you demonstrate how to use it safely before letting your child explore on his own. This section offers *Invitations to Create* for five basic tools. If you have other tools in your art space, these will give you an idea of how to set up an art prompt for any kind of tool. Have fun with it!

FIRST SCISSOR PRACTICE

(Age 2+ with adult supervision)

The first step in learning to use scissors is getting the hang of the opening and closing motion. Toddlers can practice this with plastic, toddler-safe scissors, but these scissors don't cut paper very well. That's where playdough comes in! Playdough is much easier to cut than paper and is the perfect way for young kids to practice with plastic scissors.

MATERIALS
- Playdough
- Plastic, toddler-safe scissors

SETUP
Separate the playdough into three parts. Roll two pieces into long, thin cylinders. Press one piece into a flat shape. Place the playdough and scissors alongside each other on a tray.

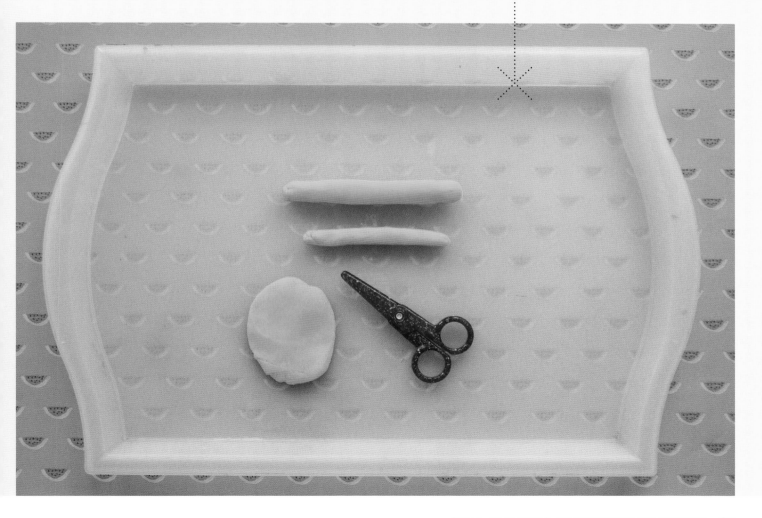

EARLY LEARNING SCISSOR PRACTICE

Once your child is ready for sharp scissors, paper is still a hard material to cut. This prompt includes two other materials that are much easier to cut than paper and will offer your child a great way practice with scissors during this beginning stage. Mardi Gras beads have a small string in between each bead that makes cutting the strand very easy for little hands. The same goes for plastic straws, which are stiff and easy to cut.

MATERIALS

- **Child-sized scissors**
- **Plastic straws**
- **Mardi Gras beads**

SETUP

Place the scissors, straws, and beads alongside each other on a tray. Mardi Gras beads and straw bits tend to fly and roll around, which is why a tray is so important.

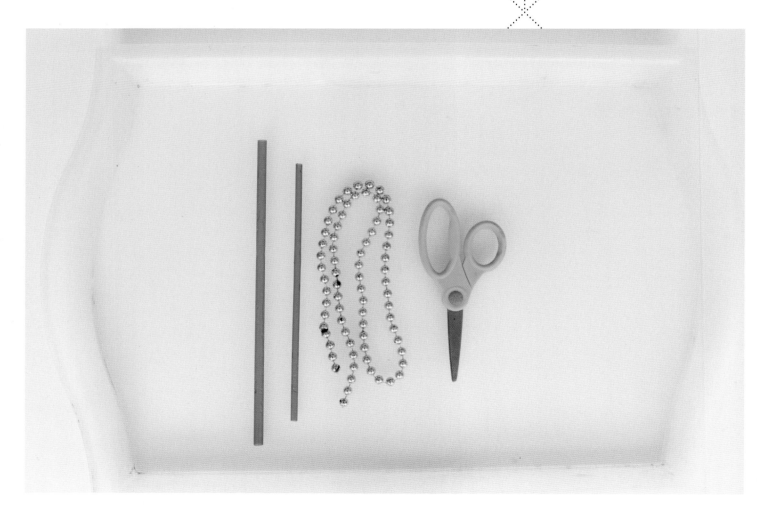

INTERMEDIATE SCISSOR PRACTICE

MATERIALS

- **Shape printout (you can find this one on page 137)**
- **Markers**
- **Child-sized scissors**

SETUP

Make a photocopy of the printout and place on a table with scissors and an assortment of markers.

After some initial practice with the previous materials, your child will be ready to cut paper. This prompt includes a printout with dotted lines. Your child may decide to draw on the printout and then try cutting along the dotted lines. Or your child may cut the paper up in a different way. That's okay!

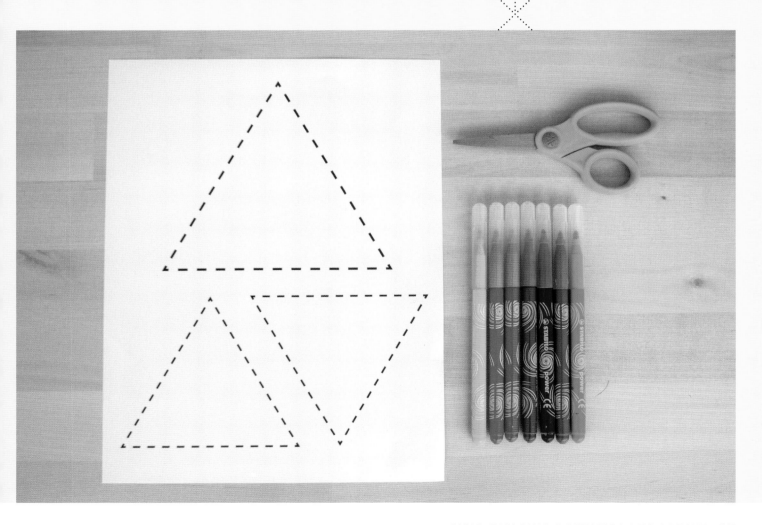

STAPLER

Kids love staplers! This prompt invites your child to draw, write, and connect the pages together with the stapler. Some kids may staple the paper into a book, while some may go staple crazy and staple the paper on all sides! Remember, there's no right or wrong way to explore the materials. Either way, your child will likely get some practice using this fun tool.

HOLE PUNCHER

This prompt involves two activities: punching holes/shapes to make confetti and gluing confetti onto a base paper. When your child is finished, save any extra confetti and add it to your art space as a new material.

TIP

Have a container on the table or nearby to collect any leftover confetti (punched holes) and add it to the materials in your art space.

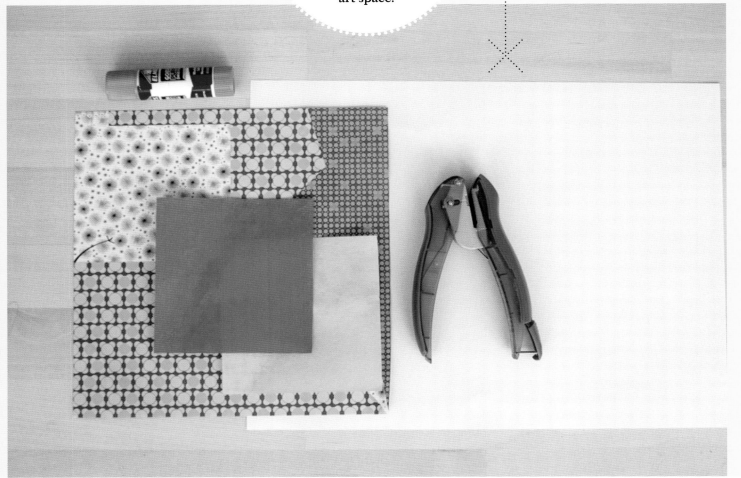

GLUE GUN

Kids love using glue guns, but it takes practice to use them safely. This prompt offers a few items from your scrap bin that are easy to glue together with a glue gun. Sit with your child the first time you offer this prompt to show her to how to handle a hot glue gun safely. Once your child gets the hang of it, this tool will likely become a favorite!

MATERIALS

- Low-temp hot glue gun
- Craft sticks/wood bits
- Recycled items (plastic lids, straws, containers)
- Glue stick (for glue gun)

SETUP

Plug in the glue gun a few minutes before your child will encounter this prompt, and place it on a table alongside the wood bits and recycled items.

TIP
Make sure to use a low-temp glue gun. If you can find one with a rubber tip, that's even better (to protect from the hot metal tip).

HAMMER

Much like a glue gun, hammers are an exciting tool for kids, but they take practice to use safely. This prompt suggests very basic materials to learn to use a hammer. Balsa wood and Styrofoam are soft materials, so they make a great base for learning to hammer a nail. Sit with your child the first time you offer this prompt to show him how to handle a hammer and nail safely.

MATERIALS

- **Hammer (child-sized)**
- **Nails (with adult supervision)**
- **Soft balsa wood or Styrofoam block**

SETUP

Place the nails in a small tray or bowl so they don't roll around. Lay the hammer and wood next to the tray of nails.

EXTEND & ENRICH

Next time you offer this prompt, add small paper shapes, tape, or oil pastels (things to decorate the wood). Your child can nail the paper shapes to the wood! Once your child has hammered in a lot of nails, you can offer string or rubber bands to wrap around the nails.

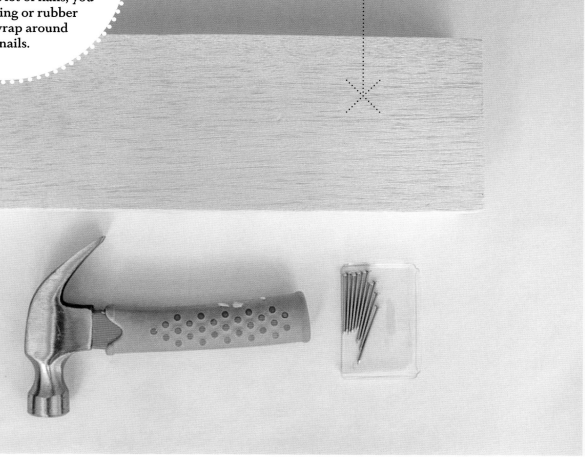

FINE MOTOR AND FOCUS

(Ages 3–6, or 2+ where noted)

Art prompts that help children develop fine motor and focusing skills

Although every *Invitation to Create* in this book will help your child develop fine motor and focusing skills, these next six prompts were included to specifically encourage this development. Fine motor development helps strengthen the muscles in little hands and is an important precursor to writing. Naturally, when a child is learning how to manipulate a tool or material with these hand muscles, a lot of focus is required. This is why the skills of fine motor and focus go hand in hand (pun intended!).

BEADING PIPE CLEANERS

(Age 2+ with adult supervision)

When kids first learn how to bead, it can be hard to poke a wobbly cord through the hole. The stiffness of a pipe cleaner, mixed with the soft outer layer, make it the perfect material to first use with beads.

MATERIALS

- **Medium-large sized beads (make sure the hole is large enough for the pipe cleaner)**
- **Pipe cleaners**

SETUP

Put the beads in a small container and place them alongside a few pipe cleaners on a tray.

TIP
If the end of the pipe cleaner is too sharp for your child, you can tightly wrap some masking tape around the end to cover the wire.

DELICATE DROPPERS

(Age 2+ with adult supervision)

Droppers (or pipettes) are a great tool to strengthen the muscles needed for a child's pincer grasp, which is the grip used in writing. It takes a little practice to understand that squeezing the end of the dropper will suck up the liquid, and how squeezing it again will release the liquid. But once kids get this concept, they love using droppers to move liquid around.

MATERIALS

- Paper towel
- Liquid watercolors (two or more colors in separate containers)
- Droppers (pipettes)

SETUP

Place the paper towel, watercolors, and droppers next to each other on a tray.

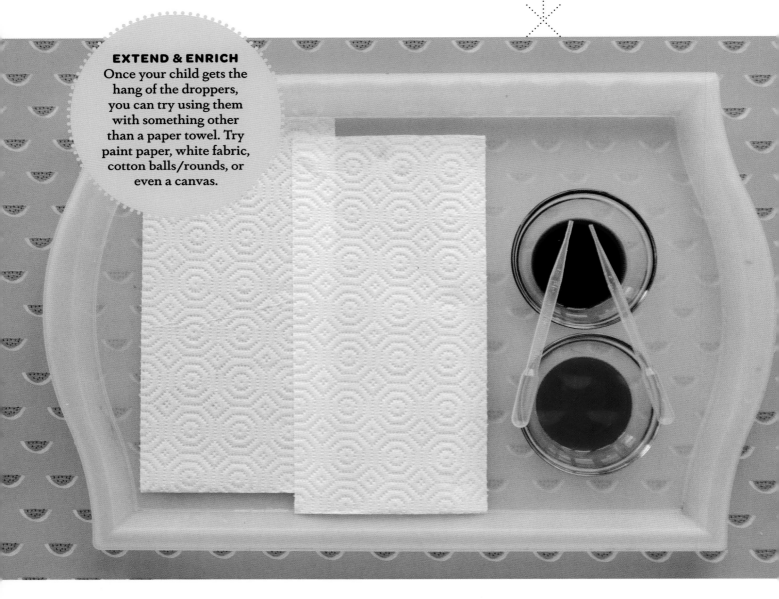

EXTEND & ENRICH
Once your child gets the hang of the droppers, you can try using them with something other than a paper towel. Try paint paper, white fabric, cotton balls/rounds, or even a canvas.

TWISTING FROM THE TOOLBOX

Twisting a nut around a bolt is a great way to strengthen hand muscles and promotes fine motor development. Kids also love using real materials from the toolbox!

MATERIALS

- **Large bolts and matching nuts**
- **Pieces of cardboard with holes (make the holes large enough to put the bolts through. A hole puncher works well for this).**

SETUP

Place the cardboard on the table alongside the nuts and bolts.

EXTEND & ENRICH

Once your child gets the hang of twisting the nuts around the bolts, you can offer other materials to attach to the cardboard (like fabric, paper, more cardboard, etc.) and either punch holes in them yourself or set out the hole puncher for your child to give it a go. You can also offer materials to decorate the cardboard like paint, markers, or oil pastels.

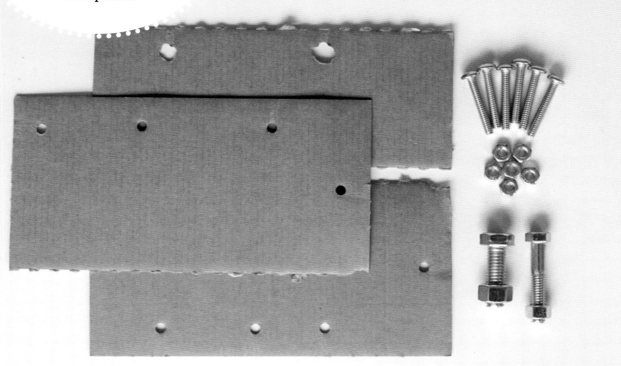

DOODAD MANDALA

A mandala (meaning *circle* in Sanskrit) is a symmetrical geometric design or pattern, most often in the shape of a circle. This prompt begins with a printout of a simple circle divided into four parts and is offered with small doodads to glue onto the paper. Your child might create something geometric or symmetrical, but he may not. Remember, there is no intended outcome with an *Invitation to Create* so see what your child comes up with!

MATERIALS

- Printout of simple circle shape/design (you can find this one at the end of the book on page 138)
- Doodads (beads, buttons, shells, gems, etc.)
- White school glue

SETUP

Place the doodads in small containers alongside the printout and glue.

LABYRINTH POINTILLISM

Following a labyrinth (either walking through one with your whole body or just moving your finger through a labyrinth) can be very calming and focusing. This prompt offers a printout of a labyrinth with paint and cotton swabs to encourage slow dot-making through the labyrinth.

MATERIALS

- **Printout of labyrinth (you can find one at the end of the book on page 139)**
- **Tempera paint (poster paint)**
- **Cotton swabs**

SETUP

Place the tray of paint with a cotton swab in each color next to the printout.

SIMPLE SEWING SKILLS

This prompt is an easy way for young kids to learn the basic up-and-down stitch motion of sewing. Your child may stitch around the edges of the paper or up and over the top and bottom of the paper. Older kids may think to connect the two papers together. Don't worry if it ends up looking like a tangled mess—that often happens with young children, and it's all part of the exploration.

MATERIALS
- **Hole-punched cards**
- **Plastic needle**
- **Yarn**

SETUP

Tie one end of yarn to the needle and the other end to one of the cards (through one of the holes). Set out on the table in an inviting way.

With the yarn attached to the card and needle, there's no need for adult intervention. Having two separate cards allows for your child to experiment with sewing the two cards together using the needle and thread.

EXTEND & ENRICH
When your child is finished exploring these materials, offer her additional paper and yarn colors to add to this creation.

SELF-SUFFICIENCY

(Ages 2–6, age 2 with adult supervision)

Art prompts that guide children towards independent use of everyday items

Becoming independent and self-sufficient is an important part of growing up and can often be overlooked with young kids. Setting up an *Invitation to Create* with materials that foster life skills is a great way to encourage self-sufficiency. When putting this book together, I thought about what my own kids and my past students have learned in the playroom that have taught them how to be self-sufficient. I came up with these five prompts that relate to art exploration, but also represent important life skills.

"Never help a child with a task at which he feels he can succeed."

—Maria Montessori

SLICING PRACTICE

Playdough is a great material to use when learning how to slice with a knife. For this prompt, you can use a toy knife, or even a plastic disposable knife if you feel your child is ready. Rolling the playdough in a cylinder or ball will get your child started.

MATERIALS

- **Playdough rolled into cylinder or ball**
- **Plastic or wooden knife**
- **Tray or cutting board**

SETUP

Place the playdough shapes alongside the knife on the tray or cutting board. You can sit with your child and demonstrate how to cut the dough with a knife or let him try on his own.

KITCHEN TOOLS

In addition to slicing, playdough can also be used with a variety of kitchen tools. You can use it with toy kitchen tools or tools from your actual kitchen. When your child begins to help out in the kitchen with real food, he will already be skilled at these particular tools!

MATERIALS
- Playdough
- Kitchen tools (spatula, rolling pin, plastic pizza cutter, cookie cutter, etc.)
- Plate

SETUP
Place the playdough onto the plate and set it alongside the tools on a table.

EXTEND & ENRICH
This could easily turn into a fun imaginative game of "restaurant" or "family." You can order something from your child and ask her to make it for you.

SQUEEZING PRACTICE

Kids love to squeeze, but they often don't want to stop! This prompt will help them learn how to dole out a small amount of paint onto a paint palette for use in their art.

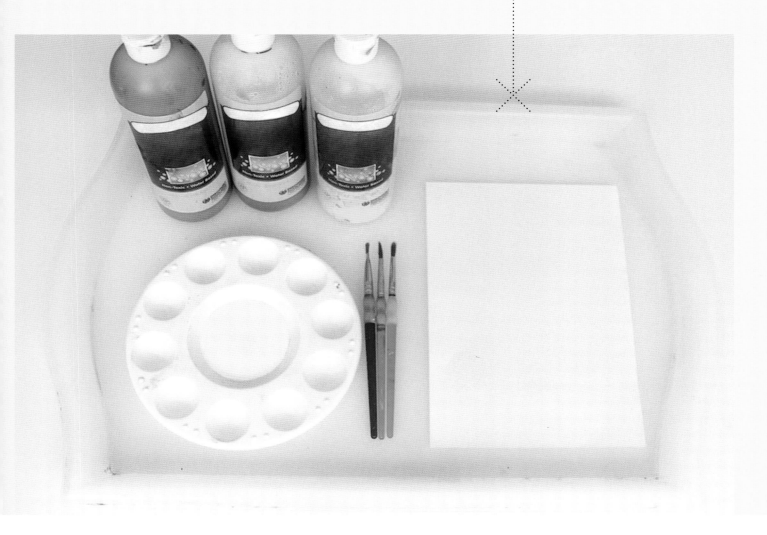

POURING PRACTICE

Pouring is a very useful skill for young kids to learn. The weight of a ceramic pitcher (rather than a lightweight, plastic one) helps children to be steady in their pouring and can also make them feel trusted.

MATERIALS

- Small pitcher of water
- Small empty cups/jars
- Small cups/jars with liquid watercolor (two different colors in their own jars)
- Paint paper

SETUP

Place the pitcher of water on a tray alongside the empty cups/jars and the paint.

They Really Will Get It

When I taught preschool, we always used ceramic or glass dishes and pitchers, and let the children serve themselves. The parents were shocked! Yet the children loved having our trust and they were always very careful. Never once did a dish or pitcher break.

ART CLEANUP

Knowing how to clean up after a messy art session is a great skill to learn at any age. It's important to clean or soak art tools before they dry so they don't get ruined. The good news is that kids often have just as much fun cleaning art tools as they do making the art! When your child is engaging in a messy art project with paint or glue, you can have a tub of warm, soapy water ready for when he is finished.

MATERIALS

- **Tub of warm soapy water**
- **Small sponge (cut a regular-sized sponge in half)**
- **Dry rag**
- **Messy art tools (after an art session)**

SETUP

When your child is done with a messy art session, invite him to help you put the messy tools in the tub of soapy water and place on a tray alongside the sponge and rag. Ask your child to help clean the tools using the sponge and explain that we need to keep the tools clean so we can use them again.

EXTEND & ENRICH
Turn this into a longer water play session by adding cups or other water toys once your child has cleaned the art tools.

WRITING *(Ages 3–8)*

Art prompts that build writing skills through playful activities

There are many ways that the practice of writing is integrated into art exploration, most often without even realizing it! All of the fine motor skills that are developed through holding tools and manipulating art materials will strengthen children's hand muscles and prime them for writing. If you want to specifically encourage your child to practice writing, these next three prompts will help build this learning into your child's play.

GREETING CARD

Making a greeting card is a really fun (and useful!) way to practice writing. Even just writing "Happy Birthday" or "Happy Holidays" is good practice. When you add markers, stickers, or any other art materials, making a greeting card is also a super fun art activity. Plus, when you have blank greeting cards stocked in your art space, you never need to purchase a ready-made card again!

MATERIALS
- Blank greeting card
- Fun stickers
- Gel pens (or fine markers)

SETUP
Place the blank card, envelope, pens/markers, and stickers on the table in an inviting way.

TIP
For a child who is learning to write, create a cheat sheet of words or phrases that your child might want to use in a greeting card (like Happy Birthday, Happy Holidays, I love you). You can put it on the table with this prompt or keep it on display in your art space for whenever your child might want to use it.

BOOK MAKING

With some paper and a stapler, you can make a simple booklet that will entice your child to write or draw inside.

MATERIALS

- Multiple sheets of paper, folded in half, and stapled to create a booklet
- Writing tools (pencil, gel pens, or fine markers)

SETUP

Place the book on the table alongside the writing tools in an inviting way.

EXTEND & ENRICH
Instead of stapling the pages together, invite your child to try sewing a book binding by punching holes along the edge and weaving yarn through the holes (then tie it off at the ends).

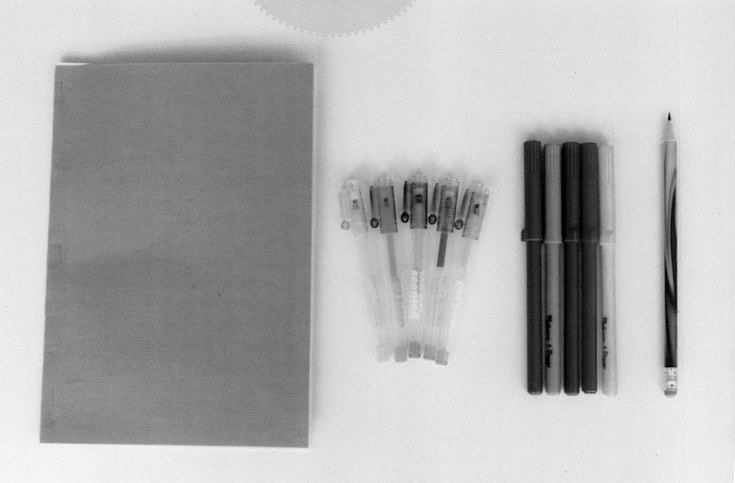

COMIC STRIP

Comic strips (or graphic novels) are a fun way to incorporate a small amount of writing practice with art and storytelling. You can start with one printout and then offer more if your child wants to continue the story on multiple pages.

MATERIALS

- Blank graphic novel/comic strip panels (you can find this printout at the end of the book on page 140)
- Colored pencils

SETUP

Place the printout alongside the colored pencils on the table.

EXTEND & ENRICH
Include a sign with a prompt to give your child ideas for a story. It could say: "Make a story about something funny that happened today," or "Make a story about someone having an embarrassing moment."

COLLABORATION

(Ages 2–10, 2 years with adult supervision)

Art prompts that encourage collaboration between siblings or friends through group projects

Collaboration happens naturally in an art space. Even when kids are working on an individual project, they still collaborate when sharing materials or asking for help. When kids come together to work on a collective project, it deepens this experience of collaboration and serves as an incredible learning opportunity for communication and teamwork. Learning how to collaborate is an important skill and can often be challenging for siblings (or even friends). The next four prompts spark collaboration and hopefully inspire you to set up collaborative art prompts on a regular basis. It can be a great way to build this skill and can also be a really fun activity for a playdate or birthday party.

SHARED STICKY COLLAGE

Contact paper has a sticky back, so it makes an easy surface to create a collage without having to use glue. You just need to use materials that are lightweight and flat so they stick well to the paper. Painting on the sticky paper adds a fun touch to this type of collage. Because contact paper comes in a roll, you can cut your paper to stretch across the entire table, which makes this a great prompt for a group of kids.

MATERIALS

- Roll of clear contact paper
- A few colors of tempera paint (poster paint) in cups
- Paintbrushes (one for each paint color)
- Small, lightweight, flat materials (tissue paper, sequins, paper shapes, glitter, etc.)

SETUP

Cut a piece of contact paper to stretch from one end of the table to the other. Peel up the corners of the film and tape the corners of the contact paper to the table with the sticky side up. You can peel off the rest of the film or leave it on the contact paper until the kids are ready to get started. Place the paint, paintbrushes, and decorative materials next to the contact paper.

TIP
When kids are done painting and collaging the contact paper, cut a second piece of clear contact paper the same length and place it, sticky side down, onto the finished artwork. The painting and collage work will then be protected and secure. Hang in a window to see how it looks with light shining through!

TAPE RESIST CANVAS

A tape resist painting is when you first place tape onto a surface before painting over it. The tape resists the paint so that when you are finished painting you can peel off the tape and see the negative space of the tape design. This is a fun activity for any age group of kids. Even if the painted area is messy, you will still see the design that the tape made once you peel it off.

SETUP

Use the painter's tape to create a word or design on the canvas. Set it out with the paints and paintbrushes on a table. Invite the kids to paint over the entire canvas, including the tape. Then peel off the tape once the painting is finished (but before the paint dries).

EXTEND & ENRICH

The next time you try this, have the kids create their own design with the tape before they paint over it.

COLLABORATIVE COLORING

This is a super simple prompt to encourage kids to create a large-scale drawing together. It's a perfect prompt to quickly set out before a playdate or for siblings to come across in the morning.

MATERIALS

- Roll of paper (a roll of easel paper or roll of butcher paper)
- Masking tape
- A few fun drawing tools (dot markers, chunky paint sticks, markers, gel pens, etc.)

SETUP

Use the masking tape to secure the paper from one end of the table to the other. Place the drawing tools on top of the paper.

SHARED STREET CONSTRUCTION

This prompt can range from simple to complex, depending on how intricate the kids want to get with their work. They may decide to make an entire neighborhood or city, which can lead to hours of building and days of play.

MATERIALS

- Large piece of cardboard
- Small cardboard items (boxes, toilet paper rolls)
- Road tape
- Masking tape
- Scissors
- Toy cars
- Toy people/animals
- Oil pastels (or crayons, markers, etc.)

SETUP

Use the large piece of cardboard as a base. Place on the table with the smaller cardboard items on top next to the road tape, masking tape, toys, scissors, and oil pastels.

EXTEND & ENRICH

Invite the kids to gather more items from the art space to add to their work. You can suggest adding fabric, yarn, wire, wood bits, decorative paper, etc. See what they come up with!

SCIENCE AND INVESTIGATION *(Ages 3–10)*

Art prompts that demonstrate the intersection of art and science through reactive ingredients, testing ideas, and exploring how things work

Most kids go wild for activities that combine art and science. They love investigating materials, playing with reactive ingredients, testing ideas, and exploring how things work. These kinds of activities also tend to be a favorite no matter the age (like the slime craze!). This makes these activities ideal for families who want to engage kids of different ages with the same materials. You'll find six prompts in this section that incorporate science and investigation. They are meant to be process-based, so allow your child to really explore and investigate what's happening with the materials. Enjoy!

EYE-CATCHING ERUPTION

This prompt is an exploration of reactive ingredients. The combination of vinegar and baking soda creates a bubbling eruption. Kids can become scientists by mixing and observing. Adding liquid watercolors to the mix creates colorful eruptions, which makes this activity even more fun!

MATERIALS

- Baking soda in a small container
- White vinegar in a small pitcher
- Empty jars
- Small measuring spoon
- Liquid watercolors (or food coloring)
- Safety glasses (optional, but it's a good practice to teach safety when experimenting with reactive ingredients)

SETUP

Place all of the materials on a tray to contain the eruptions.

EXTEND & ENRICH
Invite your child to make "potions" by adding things like glitter, flower petals, herbs, etc.

COLORFUL DRIPPING CREAM

This is an exciting prompt because of the surprising way the liquid watercolor moves through the water after it passes through the shaving cream. Kids will likely "oooh" and "ahhh" at the effect!

MATERIALS

- Tall jar, filled ¾ full with water
- Shaving cream
- Liquid watercolors in cups
- Droppers (one for each watercolor)

SETUP

Squirt a large dollop of shaving cream on top of the water in the jar. Place on a tray alongside the watercolors and droppers. Only squirt the shaving cream on the water right before your child engages with this invitation (otherwise it may melt into the water if left for too long).

EXTEND & ENRICH

If you are brave, extend this activity by offering your child the bottle of shaving cream to add to the jar after the original cream is melted by the watercolor. But be warned, this might get a little messy!

SWIRLING SEPARATION

By adding a small amount of dish soap and liquid watercolor to a shallow dish of milk, you can create swirling colors that are fun to move around and explore with a toothpick. As a scientist, your child can experiment in her own way and see what happens!

MATERIALS

- **Wide, shallow dish of full-fat milk**
- **Dish soap**
- **2 or more liquid watercolors (or food coloring)**
- **A dropper for each watercolor and one for the dish soap**
- **Toothpick**

SETUP

Squeeze some dish soap into a small cup and place it alongside the bowl of milk, toothpicks, and watercolors on a tray. Place a dropper in the dish soap and in each cup of watercolor.

NATURE STILL LIFE

As mentioned in the Current Obsession Still Life invitation (page 78), a still life drawing is an observational drawing of an inanimate object. The purpose of an observational drawing is to look closely at the shapes and lines of an object and draw what you see. Observation is an important part of both science and art. This prompt encourages kids to observe items from nature with a magnifying glass so they can draw them accurately.

(page 78)

MATERIALS

- **Nature items (shells, flowers, acorns, bark, crystals, etc.)**
- **Magnifying glass**
- **White drawing paper**
- **Pencil/colored pencils**

SETUP

Place the nature items on a table with the magnifying glass, paper, and pencil. If your magnifying glass has a stand to prop it up, place one of the nature items underneath it.

TIP
Add a sign that says something like "Draw what you see" to suggest drawing a still life.

DIY OLD-FASHIONED TEMPERA PAINT

Tempera paint was historically made using egg yolk and pigments, so this prompt is part science and part art history. Invite your child to make his own tempera paint using items from the kitchen.

EXTEND & ENRICH
Instead of using a spice to add pigment, try using powdered paint, food coloring, or graded chalk.

MAGNETIC SCULPTURE

This prompt invites kids to make a sculpture out of a mix of metal items, nonmetal items, and magnets. Kids can use the can as a base for their sculpture and explore what items will attract to the magnets. They can use the glue gun to attach the items to the base (or to the magnets) that don't attract to the magnets. Or they may do something completely different with these materials. That's the fun of *Invitations to Create*!

MATERIALS

- Metal can
- Small magnet circles
- Low-temp hot glue gun
- Random bits and bobs from your junk bin
- Small metal items (washers, nuts, bolts, paper clips, etc.)

SETUP

Set out the can, magnets, bits and bobs, metal items, and glue gun on the table in an inviting way. Plug the glue gun into a socket a few minutes before your child will work with these materials.

EXTEND & ENRICH
Include a sign that encourages making something specific like, "Make a robot out of these materials."

MAKING TOYS AND ACCESSORIES *(Ages 4–10)*

Art prompts that introduce ways to make toys or accessories that can be played with when finished

Whenever my kids are playing with their toys and they realize that they are missing a prop or accessory, they simply head to their art supplies and make it! This is one of my favorite things about having accessible art supplies in our home. It's also the reason why I have offered many opportunities for my kids to make their own toys over the years.

One way to encourage this is to set up *Invitations to Create* that can double as a toy or accessory after creation. Because I want to specifically encourage the making of things that can be played with, a few of the following prompts are a little less open-ended than other types of *Invitations to Create*. You can still set out these prompts and see what your child decides to do with them, even if it turns out completely different than expected! Or you can set out an example to show what is possible with these specific materials.

MODELING-CLAY CREATURES

Many kids love animals and love playing with toy animals. This prompt invites kids to make their own toy animals with modeling clay. Kids who have experience shaping playdough will likely be comfortable working with modeling clay. They can roll, build, twist, and attach pieces of modeling clay to make mini creatures. These creatures can then be played with after they are dry.

MATERIALS

- Modeling clay (either air-dry or bake-dry)
- Clay tools (or anything to poke and shape the clay like a toothpick, popsicle stick, etc.)
- Example of a creature made from modeling clay (optional)

SETUP

Set out the modeling clay and tools on a tray. If you think your child will benefit from seeing an example of what can be made, make an example and set it out on the tray in front of the materials.

HABITAT

This prompt can be offered as an extension of the previous one, Modeling-Clay Creatures invitation (page 123). You can entice your child to create a habitat for the creatures he made out of modeling clay by placing the creatures on the table with an assortment of materials from your art space. Alternatively, you can put a few of your child's toy animals or people on the table to jumpstart this same activity.

MATERIALS

- **Creatures from Modeling-Clay Creatures invitation (page 123) or toy animals/people**
- **Items from your junk/recycle bin**
- **Fabric**
- **Duct tape/masking tape/strong craft tape**
- **Scissors**

SETUP

Set out the creatures or toys onto the table alongside the fabric, tape, scissors, and the materials from the junk/recycle bin.

TIP
Include a sign that says something like, "Make a home for these animals."

STICKY STICKS

This is a prompt with only two types of materials, but can lead to a lot of building and playing. Once your child makes these "sticky sticks," you can save them in your art space or toy area for future play.

MATERIALS
- **Jumbo craft sticks**
- **Velcro circles (with sticky backs)**

SETUP
Make an example using two craft sticks and one set of Velcro circles. Peel off the back of the circles and attach one on one end of each stick. Then connect the two sticks together with the Velcro and set out on the table alongside the rest of the craft sticks and Velcro circles.

DIY MAGNETIC PUZZLE

Using a magnet sheet with a sticky back, your child can create a unique magnetic puzzle! Once it's finished, put this puzzle on the fridge, dishwasher, or any metal surface that will hold a magnet.

MATERIALS

- **Magnetic sheeting (with a sticky back)**
- **Drawing paper**
- **Markers**
- **Scissors**
- **Example of DIY puzzle (optional)**

SETUP

Set out the magnetic sheet, paper, markers, and scissors on the table in an inviting way. Make a sign that says something like, "Make a puzzle!" and place it next to your own example of a DIY puzzle.

DIY MUSICAL INSTRUMENT

No matter how your child combines these materials, the bells in this prompt will turn it into a jingling musical instrument that can be played with for years! Your child may discover that the wire threads through a loop on each bell. Or you can speed up this discovery in the setup (see Tip). Your child may use the tape to connect the bells or to simply decorate the stick. Or maybe she will use the tape to add an entirely new musical material to this instrument. Anything goes!

TIP
You may want to set up the materials with the wire already threaded through one of the bells. That way, your child will clearly see the possibility of using the wire to connect the bells to the stick.

Extend & Enrich
After exploring these materials, ask your child whether he can think of any other materials that may make sounds. Challenge him to create a second instrument using materials from your art space. Then have a musical jam session.

MATERIALS
- **Stick**
- **Bells**
- **Flexible wire**
- **Washi tape/craft tape**

SETUP
Tape the ends of the wire to cover sharp points. Place the materials alongside each other on the table.

DANCING PAPER DOLLS

Making paper dolls can be a blast for kids. It's exciting to design the dolls and the clothing, but add the playful element of moving limbs and your child might just play for hours with these toys.

EXTEND & ENRICH
Offer decorative paper, yarn, fabric, and glue as additional materials to decorate the doll.

MATERIALS

- **White card stock (thick paper) cut into the basic shapes of a torso, legs, arms, and head**
- **Markers**
- **Hole puncher**
- **Brads (paper fastener)**

SETUP

Lay out the body parts onto the table next to the markers, hole puncher, and brads. You can punch a hole in an upper corner of the torso and connect one of the arms with a brad if you want to show an example of how to attach the body parts to each other.

CONCLUSION

"A child is a dynamic being; art becomes for him a language of thought."
—Viktor Lowenfeld, art educator

HAVING A DESIGNATED ART SPACE IN OUR HOME

BY MERI CHERRY

Having a designated art space has changed our lives as a family. We have made art a part of our everyday in a natural and organic way because all the materials and inspiration to create are right there in front of us. I think our art space says: "Art and exploration are important to us as a family," and I like to think those ideas are paving the way for my children to be curious and confident thinkers and problem solvers in the future. I encourage everyone to find a space in their home, no matter how big or how small, to create!

"Creativity is contagious. Pass it on."
—Albert Einstein

FINAL THOUGHTS

Are you feeling inspired? I certainly hope so. I hope that this book has offered helpful information on how to set up an art playroom for kids and how to encourage open-ended, creative exploration in your new art space. But more than anything, I hope that you are inspired to reimagine art as a tool, rather than a discipline. I hope that this book has inspired you to see art as an essential form of play, of learning, and as a means to explore this fascinating world.

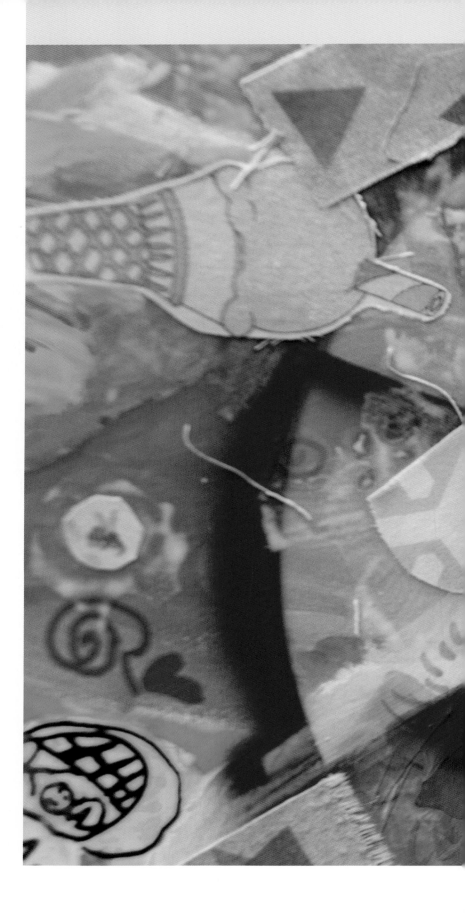

PRINTOUTS

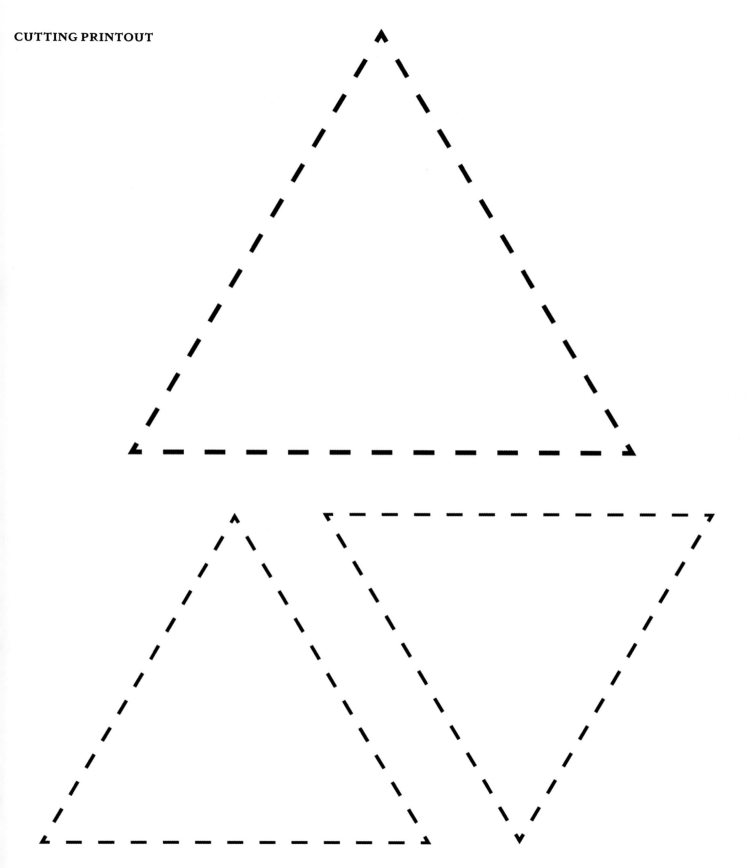

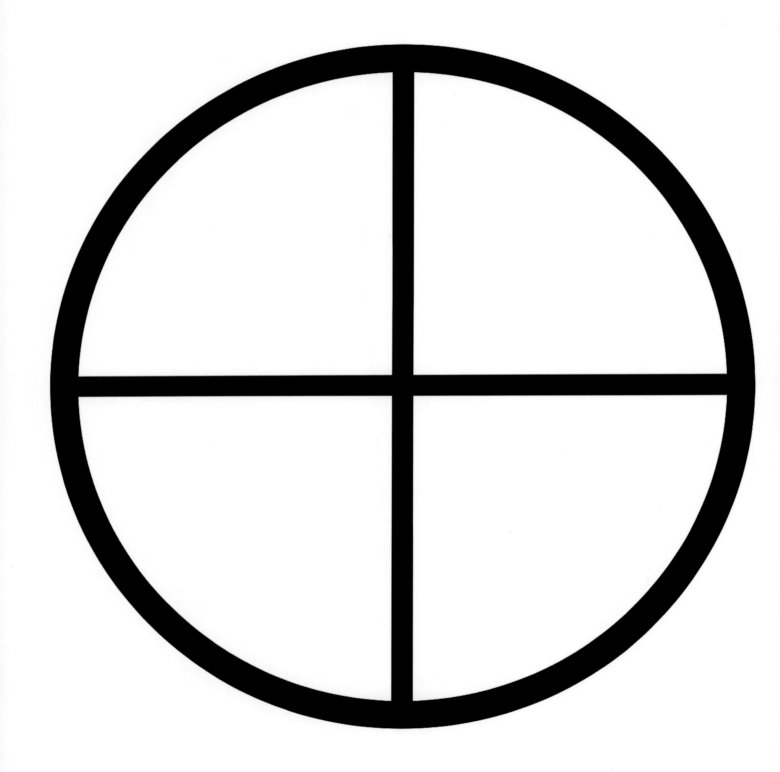

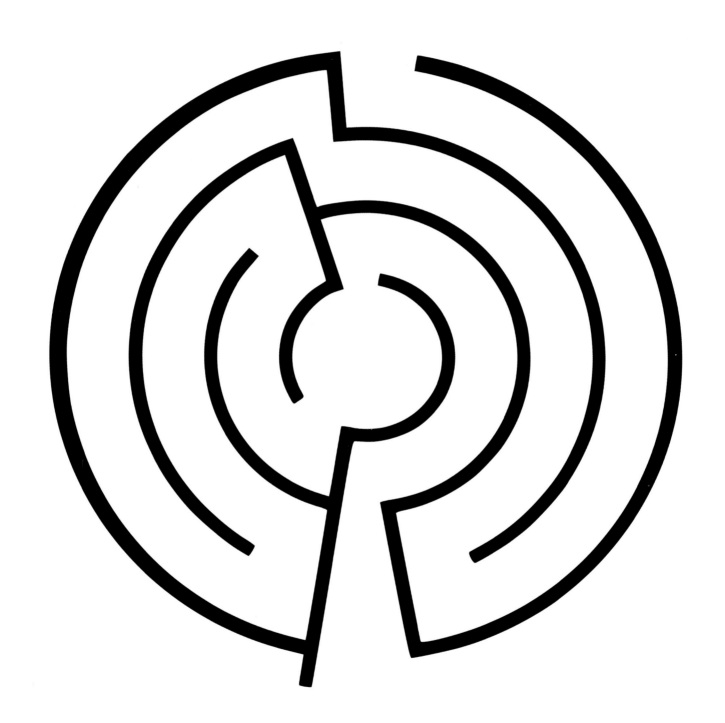

ACKNOWLEDGMENTS

This book has been years in the making and is really the culmination of my entire career working with kids in creative, educational settings. Having been in the blogging world for thirteen years, I have learned so much and been continuously inspired by friends and peers in this space. I want to first thank all the art mama bloggers and business owners out there who have not only been an inspiration, but have offered many years of support and friendship. Thank you to my students over the years, to the families who have enthusiastically engaged in (often very messy!) art with me, and to my clients who trusted me to come into their homes and dream up a creative workshop for their children. Thank you to my editor, Jonathan Simcosky, for believing in this project and seeing it through to the end. Thanks to the rest of the team at Quarto for making this a super easy process. I want to give a big thanks to the kids in this book for allowing me to snap photos while you worked and for being wide open to the creative process. You inspire me! And a special thanks to the contributors, whether it be in words or photos: Bar, Rachelle, Jean, Meri, Catalina, and Fynn. Thank you to my friends and family—especially to my parents, Joan and Mike, and my siblings, Caitlin and Scott, for your love, support, and your many roles in my creative endeavors. Thank you to Aaron for years of support and encouragement and for your continued friendship. And of course, a gigantic thanks goes to my kids, Karuna and Ora, who are my inspiration, my muses, my students, my teachers, and my collaborators. This book is for you.

ABOUT THE AUTHOR

Megan Schiller is an artist, designer, writer, and teacher. While working toward her Master's in education, Megan studied the Reggio Emilia approach to early childhood education and fell in love with the teachings on collaboration, child-led learning, and creative exploration. She took part in a study tour of the preschools in Reggio Emilia, Italy, and helped to open the first Reggio-inspired preschool in Sonoma County, California. After years of teaching preschool and running a children's art studio, Megan founded The Art Pantry, a design studio and educational resource for kids' creative spaces and art exploration. In 2017, Megan took The Art Pantry on the road in an Airstream trailer to host family art events with collaborators around the country. She recounts this creative adventure in her memoir, *Leaping Towards the Extraordinary*. Megan continues to run The Art Pantry, write, and work on her own art in the San Francisco Bay Area, where she lives with her two daughters. Megan is dedicated to helping families bring more creativity into their lives, so please contact her if you have a question. For additional resources and contact information, head over to **TheArtPantry.com.**

Photo Credit: Ora Schiller

INDEX